THE FRENCH DISPATCH

also by Wes Anderson from Faber

RUSHMORE
THE ROYAL TENENBAUMS
MOONRISE KINGDOM
THE GRAND BUDAPEST HOTEL
ISLE OF DOGS

THE FRENCH DISPATCH
OF THE LIBERTY, KANSAS EVENING SUN

screenplay by
WES ANDERSON

story by
WES ANDERSON
ROMAN COPPOLA
HUGO GUINNESS
JASON SCHWARTZMAN

faber

First published in 2021
by Faber & Faber Limited
Bloomsbury House
74–77 Great Russell Street
London WC1B 3DA

First published in the USA in 2021

Typeset by Faber & Faber Limited
Printed and bound in the UK by TJ Books Limited,
Padstow, Cornwall

A CIP record for this book is available from the British Library

ISBN 978-0-571-36047-5

FSC
www.fsc.org
MIX
Paper from
responsible sources
FSC® C013056

6 8 10 9 7 5

Contents

Nine or Ten Things I Wanted to Know about *The French Dispatch*

A conversation between
Wes Anderson and Walter Donohue

1 Where and when was the seed of the film planted? (Meaning, your interest in a literary journal as the basis for a movie.)

In Texas, when I was a teenager. Reading the *New Yorker* magazine in my school library and wondering what they were talking about.

It has been on the back burner for years and years, though, because I wasn't really coming up with any ideas for something that might actually happen at a magazine. But then I started thinking maybe the magazine in the movie might be more like a container for stories on other subjects. Which is what a magazine is, I suppose.

2 Where did the adventure begin? (Writing the movie.)

The story for this one I worked out with Roman Coppola, Hugo Guinness, and Jason Schwartzman. Hugo and I spent more time on the one about the painter. Roman and Jason and I wrote the one about the chef when we were in Italy. We all know Bill Murray, so we all had him in mind for Howitzer from the start. We figured out the Sazerac story (with Owen Wilson) at a wonderful old hotel in Rhode Island. On the seashore in winter.

3 Are there precedents for this kind of portmanteau film that you had in mind from the start? (Is it cinematic to make a movie that is actually several movies? Or is it more like television in the end?)

The very best (to me) of the anthology-type movies are the ones that were made by one director. I like *some* of the individual shorts in the sixties omnibus films – like the Fellini short in the Poe collection ('Toby Dammit' in *Spirits of the Dead*) or the Pollet story in *Paris vu par . . . .* But my real favorites are: Vittorio De Sica's *The Gold of Naples* and Max Ophüls' *Le Plaisir*.

I don't really know if it makes them more like TV episodes, but hopefully if your episodes are good enough, it doesn't necessarily make any difference?

4 *A friend of mine is a painter and I've watched as the final abstract work has slowly emerged from a figurative representation. Is this why Simone is so essential to Rosenthaler's work?*

The character of Simone in our story is sort of the crucial figure. Without her, nothing happens. The wisdom and the direction all comes from Simone.

5 *Can you describe how you and Sandro Kopp worked together to create the paintings? How did you find the words to articulate something that was abstract?*

I think I just sort of looked at what he did and tried to help him keep working on it. Step by step. Sometimes it helps to just have somebody there to say, "Try this." Because it might lead in any direction. I love what Sandro made for our story. He was good casting, I think.

He was also Tony Revolori's right hand. Literally. For all the shots of the young Moses Rosenthaler painting pictures, Sandro's arm is reaching into the frame, replacing Tony's.

6 *Would the impact of the paintings have been the same if the story had been shot in color?*

It was the Emile de Antonio movie *Painters Painting* – which I love – that suggested to me the idea to shoot only the paintings in color. Because he did that. I think, in his case, it might have been to save money on film stock for the interview parts of his film – but it is a beautiful effect. And it is such an interesting movie.

ALSO: Brian De Palma's short documentary of an opening of op art at the Museum of Modern Art – *The Responsive Eye* – in the mid-sixties. I love it, too.

7 *What was it about May '68 that made you choose that time as the context of the second story? Is it a product of all the time you've spent in Paris? Is there a personal connection?*

Mavis Gallant. That was the inspiration. Her experience of May '68 as a foreigner in Montparnasse: that especially engaged me. Our apartment in Paris is less than a block from where she lived, and I love her descriptions of the neighborhood. I love her voice and her analysis in general: clear, sharp, sometimes even bluntly judgemental – but with deep feeling and understanding. She listens, and her opinions are her own. She sees the young people not how they see themselves, not how their parents see them. She is amused, annoyed, rolls her eyes, and really does love and admire them.

*8 How did the actual menu for the kidnappers' supper emerge?
(I'm not eating radishes anymore.)*

I think, maybe, it is all a kind of twist on A. J. Liebling – but for the police.

*9 How did you devise the arrangement of the dishes so as to justify
Nescaffier's reputation as a chef par excellence?*

This was really Roman's area. He worked on each shot, each dish, to make it come to life. Our food is a bit conceptual. His cooking is more like pyrotechnics.

10 What is your favorite newsroom movie?

His Girl Friday. One of my favorites.

BUT: we also love Lewis Milestone's *The Front Page* which, as you know, remakes it in advance.

THE FRENCH DISPATCH
OF THE LIBERTY, KANSAS EVENING SUN

is dedicated to:

Harold Ross
William Shawn
Rosamond Bernier
Mavis Gallant
James Baldwin
A. J. Liebling
S. N. Behrman
Lillian Ross
Janet Flanner
Luc Sante
James Thurber
Joseph Mitchell
Wolcott Gibbs
St. Clair McKelway
Ved Mehta
Brendan Gill
E. B. White
Katharine White

Credits

Directed by
Wes Anderson

Screenplay by
Wes Anderson

Story by
Wes Anderson
Roman Coppola
Hugo Guinness
Jason Schwartzman

Produced by
Wes Anderson
Steven Rales
Jeremy Dawson

Cast and Crew

THE CONCRETE MASTERPIECE

Moses Rosenthaler	Benicio Del Toro
Julian Cadazio	Adrien Brody
J. K. L. Berensen	Tilda Swinton
Simone	Léa Seydoux
Rosenthaler Paintings by Sandro Kopp	

REVISIONS TO A MANIFESTO

Lucinda Krementz	Frances McDormand
Zeffirelli	Timothée Chalamet
Juliette	Lyna Khoudri

THE PRIVATE DINING ROOM OF THE
POLICE COMMISSIONER

Roebuck Wright	Jeffrey Wright
The Commissaire	Mathieu Amalric
Nescaffier	Stephen Park

OBITUARY

Arthur Howitzer, Jr.	Bill Murray

THE CYCLING REPORTER

Herbsaint Sazerac	Owen Wilson
Uncle Nick	Bob Balaban
Uncle Joe	Henry Winkler
Upshur "Maw" Clampette	Lois Smith
Young Rosenthaler	Tony Revolori
Prison Guard	Denis Ménochet
Chief Magistrate	Larry Pine
Waiter	Pablo Pauly
Girlfriend	Morgane Polanski
Head Caterer	Félix Moati
Mitch-Mitch	Mohamed Belhadjine
Vittel	Nicolas Avinée
Paul Duval	Christoph Waltz
Mrs. B.	Cécile de France

Mr. B.	Guillaume Gallienne
	de la Comédie-Française
Drill-Sergeant	Rupert Friend
Morisot	Alex Lawther
Mitch-Mitch (on stage)	Tom Hudson
Juliette's Friend	Lily Taïeb
Communications Specialist	Stéphane Bak
Chou-fleur	Hippolyte Girardot
Talk-Show Host	Liev Schreiber
Albert "the Abacus"	Willem Dafoe
The Chauffeur	Edward Norton
Junkie/Showgirl #1	Saoirse Ronan
Gigi	Winsen Ait Hellal
Maman	Mauricette Couvidat
Police Detective	Damien Bonnard
Patrolman Maupassant	Rodolphe Pauly
Junkie/Showgirl #2	Antonia Desplat
Hermès Jones	Jason Schwartzman
Story Editor	Fisher Stevens
Legal Advisor	Griffin Dunne
Alumna	Elisabeth Moss
Cheery Writer	Wally Wolodarsky
Proofreader	Anjelica Bette Fellini
Narrator	Anjelica Huston

Executive Producers
Scott Rudin
Roman Coppola
Henning Molfenter
Christoph Fisser
Charlie Woebcken

Director of Photography
Robert Yeoman, A.S.C.

Production Designer
Adam Stockhausen

Costume Designer
Milena Canonero

Editor
Andrew Weisblum, A.C.E.

Music by
Alexandre Desplat

Piano Solos Performed by
Jean-Yves Thibaudet

Music Supervisor
Randall Poster
"Aline" by Christophe performed by Jarvis Cocker as *Tip-top*

Hair and Make-Up Designer
Frances Hannon

Co-Producer
Octavia Peissel

Line Producer
Frédéric Blum

US Casting by
Douglas Aibel, C.S.A.

French Casting by
Antoinette Boulat

UK Casting by
Jina Jay

First Assistant Director
Ben Howard

Special Photography Unit
Roman Coppola

Additional Special Photography/Casting
Martin Scali

Unit Manager	Bertrand Girard
Animatic Editor	Edward Bursch
Key Grip	Sanjay Sami
Storyboard Artist	Jay Clarke
Gaffer	Grégory Fromentin
Costume Supervisor	Patricia Colin
First Assistant Camera	Vincent Scotet
Assistant Costume Designer	Raffaella Fantasia
Property Master	Eckart Friz
Original Music Orchestrated and Conducted by	Conrad Pope
On-Set Props	Benoit Herlin
	Till Sennhenn
Original Music Recorded and Mixed by	Simon Rhodes
Standby Carpenter	Roman Berger
Supervising Sound Editors and Re-Recording Mixers	Wayne Lemmer
	Christopher Scarabosio
Associate Producers	John Peet
	Ben Adler
Music Editor	Robin Baynton
Continuity	Jackson Malle
	Molly Rosenblatt
Sound Mixer	Jean-Paul Mugel

The FRENCH Dispatch

Obituary
(pages 1 to 9)

INSERT:

The proof-print (fresh from the press, with crop marks and registration-X's) of an obituary in the Declines and Deaths Section of a weekly newspaper magazine supplement. A line-drawing depicts an inkpot tipped over spilling a pool of black.

TITLE:

> Memorial
> "Editor-in-Chief Dead at 75"
> by the Editorial Staff

INSERT:

A caricature of a tall, bald, pudgy, bespectacled man with a pencil tucked over his ear. Caption: "Arthur Howitzer, Jr. Son of a newspaper publisher, founder of this magazine. (B: 1900, D: 1975.)"

EXT. STREET CORNER. DAY

An ash-blackened (like every facade in this French city), five story, brick and stone building of flats and *bureaux*. It lists slightly to one side. A welded metalwork sign across the upper floor reads: "The French Dispatch (of the Liberty, Kansas Evening Sun)". Down below, at street level: the magazine's delivery dock and, directly adjacent, a narrow, bustling *boîte* with a neon *Bar «Tabac» Journaux* suspended over its striped canopies. Métro station: Printer's District.

A voice (American, female, scholarly) begins:

> EDITORIAL STAFF (V.O.)
> It began as a holiday.

CUT TO:

A serving tray on a lazy-Susan. It twists left and right, back and forth, as it fills rapidly with: a *demi-tasse*, coffee in a tiny pitcher, and hot milk in a creamer; a half-bottle of cold white wine, perspiring; a crimson colored cocktail one finger deep; a short-stemmed glass of amber *aperitif*; a jigger of off-black *digestif* (which gets an egg cracked into it, two jolts of spicy sauce, and a raw oyster carefully slid from its half-shell); a small chocolate sundae; Coke in a bottle; a box of cigarettes with a book of matches; and a little glass of water with an effervescent tablet dropped in, fizzing.

> EDITORIAL STAFF (V.O.)
> Arthur Howitzer, Jr, college freshman,
> eager to escape a bright future on the
> Great Plains, convinced his father
> (more)

> EDITORIAL STAFF (V.O.) (cont'd)
> (proprietor of the Liberty, Kansas
> Evening Sun) to fund his trans-Atlantic
> passage as an educational opportunity to
> learn the family business through the
> production of a series of travelogue
> columns to be published for local readers
> in the Sunday "Picnic" magazine.

The tray booms up and sails, glass rattling but swift and sure,
away from camera on the suspended palm and fingertips of a
skilled waiter in a black waistcoat and long, white apron.

EXT. REAR COURTYARD. DAY

The *cour* of the same building. A pressboard outhouse; a coal
bin; sheaves of pulp-paper; a pile of rinds, crusts, and peels;
and a pack of pubescent schoolboys in capes, caps, and short
trousers who eat smushed *éclairs* and poke balloon-sticks at a
sleeping derelict. The café's rear door bangs open, the boys
scatter, and our waiter emerges. In a wide, vertical frame, he
speedily ascends (via three staircases, two catwalks, and a
ladder) while the obituary continues:

> EDITORIAL STAFF (V.O.)
> Over the next ten years, he assembled a
> team of the best expatriate journalists
> of his time and transformed "Picnic" into
> "The French Dispatch": a factual weekly
> report on the subjects of world politics,
> the arts (high and low), fashion, fancy
> cuisine/fine drink, and diverse stories
> of human-interest set in faraway
> *quartiers*. He brought the world to
> Kansas.

EXT. SERVICE STAIRS. DAY

A landing at the top floor. A cardboard hangs from a nail on the
door: "Silence! Writers Writing". The waiter pulls a chain-
latch, bumps the door with a cocked hip, backs inside, then
downs the bicarbonate of soda before kicking the door shut with
a thwack.

> EDITORIAL STAFF (V.O.)
> His writers line the spines of every good
> American library.

MONTAGE:

An office filled with stacked art books and clippings, walls
push-pinned top to bottom with postcards of modern art: an
unseen woman drapes a negligée over a dressing-screen.

                    EDITORIAL STAFF (V.O.)
        Berensen.

An office stocked with neatly organized galoshes, walking
sticks, hats, raincoats, boots, cameras, binoculars, notebooks,
maps, and an upside-down bicycle with a flat tire: a man on a
footstool, half off-screen, rummages on the top of a supply
cabinet.

                    EDITORIAL STAFF (V.O.)
        Sazerac.

A Spartan, white office with only a pine desk and an oak chair:
a seated woman, back to camera, smokes.

                    EDITORIAL STAFF (V.O.)
        Krementz.

An office over-decorated in scarlet, lavender, and chartreuse
with a marble torso of Adonis: a pair of espadrilled feet stick
into view propped up at the end of a chintz daybed.

                    EDITORIAL STAFF (V.O.)
        Roebuck Wright.

In the Press Room: a former-quarterback in rolled up shirt-
sleeves, hat tilted back, corrects copy in longhand with his
right hand while typing forty words per minute with his left.

                    EDITORIAL STAFF (V.O.)
        One reporter known as the best living
        writer in quality of sentences per
        minute.

In the File Room: a freckly string-bean loiters, laughing to
himself, as he reads a thesaurus and eats crackers.

                    EDITORIAL STAFF (V.O.)
        One who never completed a single article
        but haunted the halls cheerily for three
        decades.

In a formal garden (spectacularly in bloom): a tall Calcuttan in
dark sunglasses listens, nods, and takes notes with a braille
slate and stylus as a teenage, feminine amanuensis whispers in
his ear.

                    EDITORIAL STAFF (V.O.)
        One privately blind writer who wrote
        keenly through the eyes of others.

At a chalkboard: a proofreader with her hair in a bun parses a
sentence. ("They will fail to notice, under the corner of a
threadbare rug, the torn ticket-stub for an unclaimed hat which

sits alone on the upper shelf of a cloakroom in a bus depot on
the outskirts of the work-a-day town where Nickerson and his
accomplices were apprehended.")

                    EDITORIAL STAFF (V.O.)
          The uncontested crackerjack of
          grammatical expertise.

INSERT:

A right hand traces a left hand with a long calligraphy brush,
then sets to work quickly converting the outline into a gobbling
but very stylish turkey.

                    EDITORIAL STAFF (V.O.)
          Cover illustrations by Hermès Jones.

CUT TO:

A tiny man with a *frisée* of curly hair sitting at a drafting
table, pleased, as he lovingly adds feathers to his picture.

                    EDITORIAL STAFF (V.O.)
          Famously gracious with his writers,
          Arthur Jr. was less courteous with the
          rest of the magazine's staff.

Passing footsteps come to a sudden halt, and a finger jolts into
shot:

                    HOWITZER (O.S.)
          Oh, no. What's that? I need a turkey.
          Stuffed and roasted! On a table with all
          the trimmings and Pilgrims and --

CUT TO:

An accountant tallying receipts on an adding machine. An out-of-
focus figure, pacing, criss-crosses through frame in the
foreground.

                    EDITORIAL STAFF (V.O.)
          His fiscal management-system was
          convoluted but functional.

                    HOWITZER
          Give her 150 francs a week for the next
          fifteen years against five American cents
          per word, minus expenses.

CUT TO:

A door with a frosted window. Painted letters read: Editor-in-Chief. The silhouette of a standing figure listens to the silhouette of a seated one.

>   EDITORIAL STAFF (V.O.)
>   His most-repeated literary advice
>   (perhaps apocryphal) was simply this:

>   HOWITZER
>   Try to make it sound like you wrote it
>   that way <u>on purpose</u>.

EXT. TOWN HOUSE. DAY

A Queen Anne mansion on the best street of an old Mid-western, American city. In front, a uniformed chauffeur waits alongside a parked, mid-seventies hearse.

>   EDITORIAL STAFF (V.O.)
>   His return to Liberty comes precisely
>   fifty years after his departure, on the
>   occasion of his funeral, by which time
>   the magazine's circulation exceeds half a
>   million subscribers in fifty countries.

CUT TO:

An open coffin on display in the parlor. Inside: a basket tied neatly with rope, a portable typewriter, a thick stack of white paper, and a dead body (late seventies, tall, bald, pudgy, bespectacled).

>   EDITORIAL STAFF (V.O.)
>   A willow hamper containing umpteen pins,
>   plaques, and official citations of the
>   highest order is buried at his side,
>   along with an Andretti Ribbon-mate and a
>   ream of triple bond, Egyptian cotton
>   typing stock.

EXT. PRAIRIE CEMETERY. DAY

A remote graveyard in winter, late afternoon: white sky, white earth. A two-stroke excavator throttles and piston-pops, scraping at the frozen ground.

>   EDITORIAL STAFF (V.O.)
>   He received an Editor's Burial.

CUT TO:

A long corridor. The camera follows the waiter with his tray of refreshments as he searches room to room. All desks have been abandoned.

                        EDITORIAL STAFF (V.O.)
                In his will he stipulated that,
                immediately upon his death, quote:

INSERT:

A legal document labeled "Last Will and Testament". Editorial
comments, corrections, and "stets" (each initialed "A.H.Jr.")
decorate the margins in blue pencil. (Example: "Better than
melt: liquify.") Howitzer narrates this shot himself:

                        HOWITZER (V.O.)
                The presses will be dismantled and
                liquified; the editorial offices will be
                vacated and sold; the staff will be paid
                ample bonuses and released from their
                contracts; and the publication of the
                magazine will permanently cease.

CUT TO:

A stack of magazines bound in twine which thumps onto a
sidewalk. A news agent picks up the package and hangs a copy of
the final issue by a clip on the shutter of his kiosk. Cover
illustration: the spilled inkpot image now rendered in paint and
color. Caption below: 1925-1975.

                        EDITORIAL STAFF (V.O.)
                Thus, the publisher's obituary will,
                also, serve as that of this publication.
                (All home delivery readers will, of
                course, be refunded, *pro rata,* for the
                unfulfilled portion of their
                subscriptions.)

INT. EDITORIAL OFFICE. DAY

On one wall: a sun-faded map of the state of Kansas. On another:
a mock-up of the issue-in-progress with table of contents and
cards indicating articles, authors, page numbers, level-of-
completion, etc. On a table: the proofreader, frowning, one long-
stockinged leg swinging like a pendulum as she flips through
manuscript pages. On the couch: a story editor and a legal
advisor who mutter and shake their heads as they mark up
galleys. In the corner: the cheery writer, reading an almanac
and eating pretzels.

Behind his desk, arms folded, deep in thought, Howitzer looks
very much as we last saw him (in his casket), though younger by
ten years and lighter by a stone.

The waiter discreetly distributes the drinks order.

                    EDITORIAL STAFF (V.O.)
          His epitaph will be taken verbatim from
          the carved shingle fixed above the door
          of his inner office.

A *cum laude* alumna (cardigan sweater, New England accent) reads
from a spiral bound notebook, re-capping the status of the works-
in-progress:

                    ALUMNA
          Berensen's article. "The Concrete
          Masterpiece."

                    PROOFREADER
                 (coolly)
          Three dangling participles, two split
          infinitives, and nine spelling errors in
          the first sentence alone.

                    HOWITZER
                 (taking exception)
          Some of those are intentional.

There is a general murmuring. The alumna flips to the next page.

                    ALUMNA
          The Krementz story. "Revisions to a
          Manifesto."

                    STORY EDITOR
                 (darkly)
          We asked for twenty-five hundred words,
          and she came in at 14,000, plus foot-
          notes, endnotes, a glossary, and two
          epilogues.

                    HOWITZER
                 (definitively)
          It's one of her best.

Another murmuring. The alumna flips to the next page again.

                    ALUMNA
          Sazerac?

                    LEGAL ADVISOR
                 (defeated)
          Impossible to fact-check. He changes all
          the names, and only writes about hoboes,
          pimps, and junkies.

                    HOWITZER
                 (entranced)
          These are his people.

Murmuring, round three. The alumna flips the page once more,
pauses, then asks, skeptical:

> ALUMNA
> How about Roebuck Wright?

> CHEERY WRITER
> (encouraging)
> His door's locked, but I could hear the
> keys clacking.

> HOWITZER
> (firmly)
> Don't rush him.

The room erupts: bustling and chattering in a chaotic hubbub of
annoyed complaining. The alumna sips at the Coke bottle and gets
to the point:

> ALUMNA
> The question is: who gets killed? There's
> one piece too many, even if we print
> another double-issue, which we can't
> afford under any circumstances.

The room sighs and groans. Howitzer picks up the chocolate
sundae. He eats it in four decisive bites and drinks the
digestif concoction. A double-rap, then the door cracks open. A
copy boy pokes his pimply face into the room.

> COPY BOY
> Mr. Howitzer, sir? A message from the
> foreman:
> (holding up a chit)
> One hour to press.

> HOWITZER
> (instantly)
> You're fired.

> COPY BOY
> (choking-up)
> Really?

Tears stream down the copy boy's flushed cheeks. Howitzer's face
tightens. He snarls:

> HOWITZER
> Don't cry in my office.

Howitzer's index finger juts, diagonal, into the air -- pointing
to:

INSERT:

A carved shingle fixed above the door. Two words: "NO CRYING."

The copy boy reads the sign and swallows hard. He nods and exits. Howitzer shuffles the papers on his desk. He drums his fingers for ten seconds.

>   HOWITZER
>   Shrink the masthead, cut some ads, and
>   tell the foreman to buy more paper. I'm
>   not killing anybody.

The room erupts again. Howitzer wanders over to the wall where he studies the mock-up of the issue. He switches the order of the cards/articles. He switches them back, uncertain. The camera slowly zooms in on the authors' names in the table of contents.

>   EDITORIAL STAFF (V.O.)
>   Good writers. He coddled them, he coaxed
>   them, he ferociously protected them.

Howitzer looks to the waiter lingering at his side.

>   HOWITZER
>   What do you think?

The waiter shrugs. It is obvious to him:

>   WAITER
>   For myself? I would start with Mr.
>   Sazerac.

Howitzer contemplates this suggestion as the obituary concludes:

>   EDITORIAL STAFF (V.O.)
>   These were his people.

Sketchbook
(pages 11 to 17)

INSERT:

The proof-print of a weekly column in the City Section. A line-drawing depicts a Métro station entrance gate.

TITLE:

> Local Color
> "The Cycling Reporter"
> by Herbsaint Sazerac

CUT TO:

A touring bicycle with saddlebags and handlebar basket leans on its kickstand at the highest viewpoint above the smog-shrouded city. There is a clipboard steno pad mounted on the headlamp. A pencil dangles from a string.

EXT. PUBLIC SQUARE. DAY

Shuttered shops, shuttered windows, empty street. A voice (earnest, energetic, American) begins:

> SAZERAC (V.O.)
> Ennui rises suddenly on a Monday.

A stream of water surges from a storm sewer outlet-valve and rushes along a cobblestone trough, gathering candy wrappers, confetti, and cigarette butts into its current.

> SAZERAC (V.O.)
> Rusty water from the *bouches de lavage*
> slooshes down the street gutters.

Clouds of white billow from a row of exhaust pipes above a *boulangerie* as a tired worker cranks open its metal shopfront gate.

> SAZERAC (V.O.)
> Woodsmoke puffs from a hungover baker's
> chimney.

Brassieres, slips, and stockings jolt incrementally into view on a succession of pullied ropes. A cleaning lady with a cigarette dangling from her lips leans out a window, beating a rug.

> SAZERAC (V.O.)
> Leathery charwomen put out the morning's
> underthings before the air infuses with
> soot and sweat.

CUT TO:

A tall, trim cyclist, youthful but not young, dressed in a black beret with a black arm band. He holds up his pencil as he pedals up the lane addressing camera warmly. He is Sazerac.

> SAZERAC
> Through the time machine of poetic license, let us take a sight-seeing tour. A day in Ennui over the course of 250 years.

CUT TO:

Sazerac's P.O.V. with handlebars in frame.

> SAZERAC
> The great city began as a cluster of tradesman's villages.

INSERT:

A tire company road atlas of the sprawling city with encircling ring-road and suburbs. Caption: "Ennui-*sur*-Blasé, France. Population: 955,000."

> SAZERAC (V.O.)
> Only the names remain unchanged.

(Note: titles on the following before-and-after shots label them, on the left, "The Past", on the right, "The Future".)

SPLIT-SCREEN:

On the left, stalls manned by filthy street urchins brushing and polishing dozens of pairs of high-button shoes and boots; on the right, a brightly-lit, two-star inn (*Hôtel de Chaussures*) with automatic sliding-plexiglass door and a coin-operated shoeshine machine in its vestibule.

> SAZERAC (V.O.)
> The Bootblack District.

On the left, two workers lugging a cart laden with stacked masonry through a gaslit archway; on the right, an unsavory nightclub with a glowing-cursive *La Brique Rouge* over its facade.

> SAZERAC (V.O.)
> The Bricklayer's Quarter.

On the left, a glass-roofed *passage* lined with dangling carcasses (cows, pigs, horses); on the right, a subway entrance labeled *Abattoir*.

                    SAZERAC (V.O.)
          Butcher's Arcade.

On the left, a dead-end *impasse* sardine-packed with kleptos,
muggers, and hooligans; on the right, the same *impasse* sardine-
packed with punk/new-wave drug addicts.

                    SAZERAC (V.O.)
          Pick-pocket Cul-de-Sac.

MONTAGE:

An excavated construction site fifty feet deep with a parked
cement truck, stacked lumber/rebar on pallets, and dumpsters
filled with demolition-refuse. Sazerac stands on the floor of
the enormous yellow-dirt pit. The hook of a crane sways above
his head. He addresses camera again:

                    SAZERAC
          On this site: a fabled market vending all
          forms of victuals and comestibles under a
          vast, glass-and-cast-iron canopy --
          demolished, as you can see, in favor of a
          multi-level shopping center and parking
          structure.

A rumbling train car enters a tunnel and stops.

                    SAZERAC (V.O.)
          Like every living city, Ennui supports a
          menagerie of vermin and scavengers.

A view from the train car window as, outside, emergency-lights
shift on, illuminating pipes and ledges trembling with hundreds
of chestnut rats. The passengers onboard stare into space,
unfazed. (Sazerac, one hand clasping a ceiling-strap and the
other steadying his bicycle, marvels at the astonishing
infestation.)

                    SAZERAC (V.O.)
          The rats which colonized its subterranean
          railroad.

A winding block of high-angled intersecting gables and parapets
vibrating with hundreds of mangy alley cats. (Sazerac, poking up
from a skylight window, sets out a saucer of milk.)

                    SAZERAC (V.O.)
          The cats which colonized its slanty
          rooftops.

A shallow, stone waterway only two meters wide zig-zagging the
gaps between disused brick storehouses. Workers criss-cross
flexing planks above the dark water. (Sazerac dips a mini-net

from a pocket fishing-kit, scoops up a clump of wiggling
bootlace eels, and eats a handful, raw.)

>   SAZERAC (V.O.)
>   The *anguillettes* which colonized its
>   shallow drainage canals.

The previously-seen schoolboys, now crouched behind a parked
Citroën delivery van, eat smushed creampuffs, then spring upon
an old lady rolling a basket of groceries up the sidewalk and
poke balloon-sticks at her. She shouts, furious, and swats
violently with her cane until the boys scatter away.

>   SAZERAC (V.O.)
>   After receiving the Host, marauding
>   choirboys (half-drunk on the Blood of
>   Christ) stalk unwary pensioners and seek
>   havoc.

A terraced cemetery densely dotted with tombs and markers. At
the foot of a modest crypt (labeled, under a weeping angel,
"Lucette Sazerac, 1920-1955"), Sazerac arranges a little meal,
spread neatly across a rectangle of wax paper, and dines in
silence.

>   SAZERAC (V.O.)
>   A typical worker's-lunch.

A bi-level street with a steep stone staircase leading from a
used bookstore down to a packed café surrounded by mopeds and
scooters.

>   SAZERAC (V.O.)
>   In the Flop Quarter: students. Hungry,
>   restless, reckless.

A hunchbacked, old man with a cane, a bag of medicine, and a
muffler around his neck waits next to a bench on a lonely
street. A bus arrives, the door opens, and the old man slowly
attempts to bring his foot up to the bottom step.

>   SAZERAC (V.O.)
>   In the Hovel District: old people. Old
>   people who have failed.

Sazerac grips a handrail at the rear of a Citroën diaper-service
delivery *camionette* as it pulls him swiftly down a congested
boulevard on his bicycle. He addresses camera again:

>   SAZERAC
>   The automobile: a mixed blessing. On the
>   one hand: the honking, skidding,
>   speeding, sputtering, and backfiring; the
>   emission of toxic fumes and filthy
>   (more)

> SAZERAC (cont'd)
> exhaust-pollution; the dangerous
> accidents; the constant traffic; the high
> cost of --

The road splits, unexpectedly, and Sazerac (shocked for an instant) jangles down a short staircase, disappearing out of frame, to an unseen crash-site below.

> SAZERAC (V.O.)
> Department of local statistics:

In a pouring rain: a long, blank, stone wall extending straight up out of frame as far as visible. Painted on it: "Prison/Asylum."

> SAZERAC (V.O.)
> Average rainfall: 750mm.

In a falling snow: a *pissoir* consisting of a shoulder-level metal privacy screen circling a dirty fountain. Painted on it: "Public Urinal."

> SAZERAC (V.O.)
> Average snowfall: 190,000 flakes.

A dockworker extends a long pole into the water and drags a face-down, floating corpse toward the shore.

> SAZERAC (V.O.)
> 8.25 bodies are pulled from the *Blasé*
> river each week (a figure which remains
> consistent despite advances in health and
> hygiene).

Well-dressed prostitutes, alone and in pairs, linger in their habitual locations (under a streetlamp, next to a cigarette machine, outside a strip-club stage door).

> SAZERAC (V.O.)
> As the sun sets, a medley of unregistered
> streetwalkers and gigolos replaces the
> day's delivery boys and shopkeepers, and
> an air of promiscuous calm saturates the
> hour.

Competing performers (strongman, fire-eater, old woman warbling a torch song) entertain a crowd along the riverside. In the distance: laughter, breaking glass, a gunshot, a scream.

> SAZERAC (V.O.)
> What sounds will punctuate the night, and
> what mysteries will they foretell?

Sazerac appears to struggle for control of the bicycle as he
dodges potholes. He disappears behind a bookseller's stall and
shouts in pain/confusion. His bicycle, surprisingly balanced,
immediately reemerges (at speed), now riderless.

                    SAZERAC (V.O.)
          Perhaps the doubtful old maxim speaks
          true:

Sazerac carries his bicycle over his shoulder down the sidewalk
as the sky darkens from blue to black and the lights of the
neighborhood twinkle on. The front wheel is bent and twisted
like a coat hanger.

                    SAZERAC (V.O.)
          All grand beauties withhold their deepest
          secrets.

INT. WRITER'S OFFICE (SAZERAC). DAY

On the floor: Sazerac repairs his upturned bicycle. In the
corner: the cheery writer reads a dictionary and eats peanuts.
At the desk: Howitzer scrutinizes a proof-print, muttering/
quoting under his breath:

                    HOWITZER
          "Rats, vermin, gigolos, street
          walkers..."

Howitzer interrupts himself, looking over his glasses:

                    HOWITZER
          You don't think it's almost too seedy
          this time? For decent people.

                    SAZERAC
               (slightly offended)
          No, I don't. It's supposed to be
          charming.

Howitzer nods, unconvinced. He shuffles to another page and
resumes his muttering/quoting:

                    HOWITZER
          "Pick-pockets, dead bodies, prisons,
          urinals..."

Howitzer interrupts himself (looking over his glasses) again:

                    HOWITZER
          You don't want to add a flower shop or an
          art museum? A pretty place of some kind.

SAZERAC
(slightly more offended)
No, I don't. I hate flowers.

Howitzer nods again, reluctant but resigned. Sazerac tightens a
spoke. Howitzer shrugs.

HOWITZER
You could cut the second half of the
second paragraph, by the way. You already
repeat it later.

Howitzer holds up the manuscript and points to a bracketed
passage. Sazerac, suspicious, squints. Pause.

SAZERAC
OK.

Howitzer crosses out the section of text with a blue pencil.

Story #1
(pages 19 to 57)

INSERT:

The proof-print of a biographical profile in the Arts and
Artists Section. A line-drawing depicts a painter's easel.

TITLE:

> Studio Portrait
> "The Concrete Masterpiece"
> by J.K.L. Berensen

(Note: the following chapter of the film is presented in black
and white with the exception of: 1. the latter-day cutaways to
Berensen's talk at a museum in Kansas; and 2. Rosenthaler's work
itself, which always appears in color within the black and white
scenes.)

INT. RECREATION ROOM. DAY

A white-washed hall the size of a squash court. Walls and
ceiling are stained with damp and mold and plastered in concrete-
render. Floors are stone, dirt, and mortar. A female model
(Simone, age thirty) stands naked on a table, legs apart, feet
flat, arms behind her back, frozen in an exceedingly
uncomfortable pose. Across the room: a shirtless painter (Moses
Rosenthaler, age fifty) in short-shorts and clogs works in oil,
briskly and diligently. His body is barrel-chested; his face is
thick-bearded; and, from head to toe, he is strikingly paint-
splattered. (We see only the back of the medium-sized canvas.)

Rosenthaler pauses and examines his picture. He crosses the room
and stares, close-up, at Simone. He grips her arms and firmly
draws them back, taut. She frowns slightly. He daubs paint onto
the side of her stomach with his brush. He blots color from his
palette then daubs at her stomach again. He smudges the paint
into her skin with his fingers. He studies the two pigments (oil
paint and human flesh). Simone narrows her eyes and bites her
lip. Rosenthaler blots to adjust the chroma once more -- but
just before he can daub at Simone a third time, she slaps him
hard across the face. Rosenthaler recoils, stumbling, scampers
across the floor, and returns to his canvas where he immediately
resumes his efforts.

Simone holds her pose.

A loud bell rings, a loud buzzer buzzes. Rosenthaler immediately
lowers his brush and begins to organize his paints and
turpentines into a tool box. Simone disappears behind a wooden
panel and pulls a garment down from a hook. Rosenthaler
disappears behind a storage locker, pulls off his short-shorts,
and washes himself with an industrial hose and scrub-brush.

(Note: the splattered-paint does not come off; in fact,
Rosenthaler always appears fully splattered, at all times, in
some form of pigment or medium.)

Simone re-emerges, now dressed in the uniform of a prison guard
with black baton swinging at her waist. She finishes fixing her
hair and tightens her belt. Rosenthaler re-emerges, now dressed
in a prisoner's tunic with text stenciled on the back: *Condamné
Psychopathe*. He finishes drying himself with a toweling-rag.

Simone slips Rosenthaler's arms into a straitjacket, clips the
bindings, clanks open an iron-barred door, and directs the
patient/inmate/artist out of the room. The door closes, locks,
and latches. Silence.

The camera dollies across the empty space, past the table, the
wooden panel, the storage locker, to finally reveal the recto of
Rosenthaler's unfinished painting: a thickly encrusted, oily
impasto; almost totally abstract; flesh from the tube sculpted
and schmeared with red, orange, and yellow skylight; slashed on
one side with a black, blue, and purple border of tangled barbed-
wire and shattering glass; Simone, unrecognizable, is
nevertheless present in every brushstroke.

INT. MUSEUM AUDITORIUM. NIGHT

The spotlit proscenium of a modernist assembly hall. Projected
on a screen above the stage: a black and white mug-shot/slide of
Rosenthaler, paint-splattered. A woman of-a-certain-age
(American, hair-sprayed *coiffure*, *couture* dress) stands at the
lectern with a wired remote-switcher clasped in her hand. She is
poised, enthusiastic, and vibrantly engaging. She is J.K.L.
Berensen.

An attentive audience listens in the dark.

> BERENSEN
> We take as the subject of tonight's
> lecture the great painter at the vanguard
> of the French Splatter-school Action-
> group, Mr. Moses Rosenthaler. Widely
> celebrated, as you know, for the bold,
> dramatic style and colossal scale of his
> middle-period -- in particular, of
> course, the polyptych-tableaux known as
> "Ten Reinforced Cement Aggregate (Load-
> bearing) Murals" -- he remains, in my
> opinion, the most eloquent (and,
> certainly, the loudest) artistic voice of
> his rowdy generation.

Berensen clicks the remote-switcher, and further black and white
slides flip into view showing a panorama-view of ten panels,
each sixteen feet tall, which continue and expand the themes of

thickly encrusted flesh, tangled barbed-wire, shattering glass, etc.

> BERENSEN
> How does this pivotal piece come to find
> its way into its unique position as a
> permanent installation here at the
> Clampette Collection? The story begins in
> a mess hall.

INT. PRISON CAFETERIA. DAY

A catwalk around the upper perimeter of a cinder-block lunchroom which serves as the viewing platform for a presentation of rudimentary, primitive artworks: a fingerpainting of a tree, a *papier mâché* cactus, a wastebasket fashioned from bound twigs, etc. -- plus Rosenthaler's portrait of Simone, now complete and varnished. A small number of prisoners and guards wanders from piece to piece, perusing and puttering. One prisoner, however, appears to be utterly transfixed by the painting (mentioned above) under his inspection. He is forty, clean-shaven, well groomed; wavy, silver hair, sharply parted; prison uniform, neat and pressed. He is Julian Cadazio.

> BERENSEN (V.O.)
> The exhibition "Ashtrays, Pots, and
> Macramé" (a group show of handicrafts by
> amateur artisans incarcerated in the
> lunatic section of the Ennui Prison/
> Asylum) might, perhaps, have been omitted
> from the annals of art history had it not
> been for the inclusion in its number of a
> small painting by Mr. Rosenthaler (who
> was, at that time, serving a fifty year
> sentence for the crime of double-
> homicide), and the observation of that
> work by a fellow inmate, the Levantine
> art dealer Mr. Julian Cadazio (who, by
> fateful coincidence, happened to be
> imprisoned in the adjoining annex on a
> charge of second-degree sales tax
> evasion).

Cadazio signals to a nearby, pot-bellied, wall-eyed guard:

> CADAZIO
> Guard.

Cadazio's manner lacks any inkling of subservience. The guard reluctantly makes the effort to look up. He waits. Cadazio's eyes have not left the canvas, but in one extended hand: there is a gold foil enveloped *marron-glacé* in a fluted paper candy-cup.

                    CADAZIO
          Who painted this picture?

Pause. The guard slowly approaches, snatches the *bonbon* into his
mouth, peers at a small label next to the painting, then studies
a corresponding list.

                    GUARD
          Citizen 7524.

                    CADAZIO
          I believe that unit designates Maximum
          Security for the Demented and Deranged.
          Are you able to provide me an escort and
          a Friendly Visit Stamp? For immediate
          use.

The guard scoffs -- then hesitates. In Cadazio's re-extended
hand: three more *marron-glacés.*

INT. LOCK-UP CORRIDOR. DAY

Cadazio follows the guard down a wide passage segmented by
consecutive, iron-barred gates.

INT. CELL BLOCK. DAY

A tiny bedroom of extreme austerity: burlap hammock, cracked and
yellowed ceramic washbasin, coiled radiator in the corner,
padded walls. Rosenthaler and Cadazio face each other seated on
low footstools. Simone stands outside the cage-door with a ring
of skeleton keys in her hand.

                    CADAZIO
          "Simone, Naked, Cell Block J. Hobby-
          room." I wish to buy it.

Rosenthaler reacts subtly but at some length (surprise,
suspicion, confusion, a hint of sad pride), looks to Simone,
then says to Cadazio simply:

                    ROSENTHALER
          Why?

                    CADAZIO
               (simply)
          Because I like it.

                    ROSENTHALER
               (simply)
          It's not for sale.

                    CADAZIO
                (dismissive)
        Yes, it is.

                    ROSENTHALER
                (uncertain)
        No, it's not.

                    CADAZIO
                (certain)
        Yes, it is. All artists sell all their
        work. It's what <u>makes</u> you an artist. If
        you don't plan to sell it, don't paint
        it. The question is: what's your price?

Cadazio stares hard into Rosenthaler's wounded eyes. Rosenthaler
stares back at Cadazio's poker-face -- then looks to Simone
again before he mumbles:

                    ROSENTHALER
        Fifty cigarettes.
                (on second thought)
        Actually, make it seventy-five.

                    CADAZIO
                (frowns)
        Why do you keep looking at that guard?

Pause. Rosenthaler says inevitably:

                    ROSENTHALER
        She's Simone.

                    CADAZIO
                (hesitates)
        Ah.

Cadazio slowly turns to Simone. Simone looks back at him evenly.
Cadazio nods, looks back to Rosenthaler, and says crisply:

                    CADAZIO
        I don't want to buy this important piece
        for fifty cigarettes --

                    ROSENTHALER
        Seventy-five.

                    CADAZIO
        -- or seventy-five of prison currency. I
        want to pay you 250,000 francs in legal
        French tender. Do we agree? On the sale.

Rosenthaler's eyes widen. He and Cadazio both now look to
Simone. Simone, mightily impressed, says softly:

SIMONE
Uh-huh.

Cadazio digs into his pockets for a handful of coins and
cigarettes plus his last *marron-glacé* as he explains:

CADAZIO
I can only offer a deposit of --
(counting coins)
-- 83 *centimes,* one candied-chestnut, and
<u>four</u> cigarettes (everything I have), at
this present moment; however, if you'll
accept my signatory-voucher, I assure
you, a check for the outstanding balance
will be remitted to your account within
ninety days. Where do you bank? Never
mind.

Cadazio scribbles on a business card and hands it to
Rosenthaler. Rosenthaler jabs one cigarette into his mouth,
passes the second to Cadazio, sticks the spares under the
elastic of his sock -- then presents the sweet to Simone. She
eats, they smoke. Cadazio asks bluntly:

CADAZIO
How'd you learn to do it, by the way?
Paint this kind of picture. Also: who did
you murder (and how crazy are you,
really)? I need background information so
we can do a monograph. It makes you more
important.
(expansively)
Who <u>are</u> you --

Cadazio leans forward and reads from a tin dog-tag hanging from
a string around Rosenthaler's neck:

CADAZIO
-- Moses Rosenthaler?

CUT TO:

The museum auditorium. Berensen is at her lectern. On the
screen: a turn-of-the-century photograph of a bearded, well-to-
do man seated bareback on a massive stallion alongside a very
small boy on a very small pony.

BERENSEN
Born rich, the son of a Jewish-Mexican
horse rancher, Miguel Sebastien Maria
Moisés de Rosenthaler trained at the
École des Antiquités at significant
family expense; but, by the end of his
youth, he had shed all the luxuries of
(more)

                        BERENSEN (cont'd)
            his comfortable background and replaced
            them with:

MONTAGE:

A filthy garret apartment with skylight windows, four unmade
beds (one occupied by an unconscious, face down woman), and
three artists at easels, all painting still-lifes. Among them is
young Rosenthaler (played by a younger actor), already paint-
splattered (though in softer hues), holding a bottle of beer in
the same hand as his brush.

                        BERENSEN (V.O.)
            Squalor.

A footbridge busy with tourists. Young Rosenthaler paints the
river view while holding a bottle of wine in the same hand as
his brush. A passer-by drops a coin into his upturned hat.

                        BERENSEN (V.O.)
            Hunger.

A boxcar clacking along a curving track above a sunflower field.
Young Rosenthaler, in hobo rags, paints a flea-bitten dog while
holding a flask of whiskey in the same hand as his brush.

                        BERENSEN (V.O.)
            Loneliness.

The terrace of a white stone desert fort. Young Rosenthaler, in
khakis and *kepi*, paints a seated officer while holding a snifter
of cognac in the same hand as his brush. A whizzing bullet
pierces the canvas, and the company scrambles for weapons and
cover -- except Rosenthaler, who continues calmly at his canvas.

                        BERENSEN (V.O.)
            Physical danger.

A weedy cloister with stone walls and scattered pebbles. Young
Rosenthaler, naked, his dark-shadowed eyes bloodshot and
deranged, paints a self-portrait in a hand mirror while holding
a beaker of *eau-de-vie* in the same hand as his brush.

                        BERENSEN (V.O.)
            Mental illness.

A dockside tavern. Young Rosenthaler, in sleeveless undershirt,
paints a picture of an absinthe bottle while holding a glass of
its contents in the same hand as his brush.

                        BERENSEN (V.O.)
            And, of course, criminal violence.

At the other end of the bar, two hulking, smirking bartenders lean on the counter in front of a weathered, elderly man, needling him. The old man is stoic. Young Rosenthaler watches like an animal. Under his breath, almost inaudibly but unmistakably: he growls. The camera dollies to a kitchen door porthole where a scullery boy renders (with a meat-saw) the hanging carcass of a slaughtered calf.

> BERENSEN (V.O.)
> He did not pick up a brush during the
> first decade of his long prison sentence.

A padded prison cell. Young Rosenthaler, splattered in machine-grease, pours a single shot from a bottle labeled Mouthwash *de Menthe* (150 proof). Off-screen: a latch clanks. Young Rosenthaler looks up. He rises from his stool and makes way as his older self, identically dressed and splattered, enters and (with a gentle acknowledgement, eye to eye, of the boy he once was) takes the seat. Young Rosenthaler removes the dog-tag from around his own neck and loops it over older Rosenthaler's head. Young Rosenthaler exits. Older Rosenthaler sips the mouthwash and stares at the blank walls.

TITLE:

> Year 11, Day 1

INT. CRAFTS STUDIO. DAY

A basement classroom. Simone sits at a metal desk next to the door. Fifteen prisoners shuffle past her and file into rows of benches behind footstools prepared with various pottery-making supplies. Rosenthaler enters last. He pauses in front of Simone and says quietly:

> ROSENTHALER
> Permission to sign up for Activity-
> privileges, *gardienne*.

> SIMONE
> (without looking up)
> You have a Registration chit?

> ROSENTHALER
> (hesitates)
> This thing?

Rosenthaler digs into his pockets. He produces a small, thin ticket and holds it up, uncertain. Simone tears the corner and gives it back to him. As Rosenthaler begins to move toward his seat -- Simone stops him with an announcement:

                    SIMONE
          Attention. We have a new convict joining
          us today. Citizen 7524, address the
          class.

Rosenthaler, startled, speaks under his breath:

                    ROSENTHALER
          What do you mean?

                    SIMONE
          Tell the group about yourself.

                    ROSENTHALER
          I don't want to do that.

                    SIMONE
          It's mandatory.

                    ROSENTHALER
          They know me already.

                    SIMONE
          That's not the point.

                    ROSENTHALER
          I didn't prepare any speech.

                    SIMONE
               (an official order)
          Say something.

Rosenthaler looks stricken. Simone nods for him to speak. He
turns to the room. He gathers his thoughts. Finally, he begins:

                    ROSENTHALER
          I've been here 3647 days and nights.
          Another 14,603 to go. I drink fourteen
          pints of mouthwash-rations per week. At
          that rate, I'm going to poison myself to
          death before I ever see the world again,
          which makes me feel -- very sad. I've got
          to change my program. I've got to go in a
          new direction. Anything I can do to keep
          my hands busy: I'm going to do it.
          Otherwise, I think maybe it's going to be
          a suicide. That's why I signed up for
          Clay Pottery and Basket Weaving. My name
          is Moses.

Troubled convicts (shorn heads, crooked noses, combat scars)
stare at Rosenthaler. His hard face is streaked with tears.
Simone says simply:

                         SIMONE
            Take a pew.

Simone points. Rosenthaler looks to: a hunk of wet clay on a
footstool in front of an empty seat at the back of the room.

CUT TO:

Five minutes later. The entire class of convicts has gathered to
watch, intrigued, as Rosenthaler briskly, nimbly, expertly
sculpts. Rosenthaler pauses to study his work. He twists the
sculpture around for everyone to see.

INSERT:

A hasty but magnificent vase with bas-relief depicting a bouquet
of wildflowers with wind-blown petals floating in the air and a
crane standing on one leg. Simone descends into the shot and
studies the vessel -- impressed, then suddenly and deeply moved.
Rosenthaler asks softly:

                    ROSENTHALER (O.S.)
            What's your name, *gardienne*?

Simone looks up to Rosenthaler. Her lips move, but her voice is
inaudible under Berensen's:

                    BERENSEN (V.O.)
            Certain women do gravitate toward
            incarcerated men. It's a recognized
            condition.

Rosenthaler's rough, clay-splattered hand enters frame with a
blade of straw pinched between two fingers, and, in one rapid,
sure effort: cuts a beautiful, extravagantly-filigreed letter
"S" into the wet clay on a cloud above the etched flora.

CUT TO:

Berensen at her lectern.

                    BERENSEN
            Something about the captivity of others
            enhances the experience of their own
            freedom. I assure you, it's erotic. Look
            at her, by the way.

Berensen remote-switches through a succession of black and white
slides of Simone: at fourteen, with numerous siblings, reaping
in a wheat field; at sixteen, pregnant, plucking a goose; at
eighteen, not pregnant, skinning a rabbit; at twenty, in a
nurse's uniform on a battlefield with soldiers advancing and
retreating in the background.

(Note: in each of these images, all other subjects, human and
animal, are blurry; only Simone holds completely still for the
photograph.)

> BERENSEN
> Born into quasi-serfdom. Sixteen brothers
> and sisters. Illiterate until she was
> twenty. Now a woman of considerable
> property. Radiant.

Paused on the screen: an image of a somewhat younger, paint-
splattered, naked Berensen caught reaching for a dressing gown.
Berensen finally notices and mutters, startled:

> BERENSEN
> Good God. Wrong slide. (That's me.)

Berensen remote-switches back to Simone at eighteen, briskly re-
composes herself, and carries on:

> BERENSEN
> Simone, of course, refused all
> Rosenthaler's entreaties of marriage
> (which, we are told, were frequent and
> marvelously enthusiastic).

INT. LAUNDRY ROOM. NIGHT

Midnight. Rosenthaler and Simone, motionless and naked, recline
on a heap of bed linens and dishrags in a deep pile on the
floor. Berensen continues:

> BERENSEN (V.O.)
> She insists to this day (I'm going to
> quote from her finely-written memoir): "I
> never belonged to Moses Rosenthaler. Not
> for a single day, not for a single hour.
> I merely bore him a warm, deeply
> affectionate esteem."

In the meantime, Rosenthaler has been searching for the words to
begin the scene:

> ROSENTHALER
> I want to say it as simple as I can. To
> try to shape it into words. The feelings
> in my heart.

Simone and Rosenthaler say simultaneously:

ROSENTHALER	SIMONE
I love you.	I don't love you.

                    ROSENTHALER
                 (frowning)
          What?

                    SIMONE
          I don't love you.

                    ROSENTHALER
                 (hesitates)
          Already?

                    SIMONE
                 (blankly)
          Already what?

                    ROSENTHALER
          Already how do you know that? How can you
          be sure? So quick.

                    SIMONE
                 (with certainty)
          I'm sure.

                    ROSENTHALER
                 (wounded)
          Ouch. That hurts me. The cruelty of it.
          The cold-bloodedness.

                    SIMONE
          You said what you wanted to say. I tried
          to stop you. That's it.

                    ROSENTHALER
          I said part of what I wanted to say. I
          was in the middle of it. There's more.

Silence. Rosenthaler attempts to propose marriage:

                    ROSENTHALER
          Will --

                    SIMONE
                 (interrupting)
          No.

                    ROSENTHALER
          Will you --

                    SIMONE
                 (interrupting)
          No.

                    ROSENTHALER
          Will you marry --

                         SIMONE
                    (interrupting)
          Should I put you in your straitjacket,
          take you back to your cell, and lock you
          up again?

Rosenthaler sighs. He digs out a bottle of mouthwash from the
tangled linens and takes a sip. Simone frowns. Rosenthaler
explains:

                         ROSENTHALER
          It's diluted.

Pause. Simone produces a child's sock from a knitted sack and
begins to darn it. Rosenthaler looks up and stares into the
camera. His face lightens.

CUT TO:

Rosenthaler's P.O.V. of the ceiling. Purple soot blackens its
edges and corners. Nicotine yellows its cracked plaster. Rusty
water stains speckle all across in faded flesh-tones. Decades of
pollution and decay meld into a spectacular visual pandemonium.

Rosenthaler says, transported:

                         ROSENTHALER
          I need art supplies (canvas, stretchers,
          paints, brushes, turpentine).

                         SIMONE
                    (continuing to darn)
          What do you want to paint?

                         ROSENTHALER
          The future.

Rosenthaler turns to look into Simone's eyes. He says
profoundly:

                         ROSENTHALER
          Which is you.

CUT TO:

Berensen at her lectern again.

                         BERENSEN
          Widely not considered a great
          connoisseur, Julian Cadazio,
          nevertheless, had an eye for something,
          and he did us all a very good turn when,
          the hour he was released from prison --

EXT. ART GALLERY. NIGHT

A storefront situated on a brief cul-de-sac over the river.
Beveled letters above the door identify it as: "Cadazio Uncles
and Nephew *Galerie* (Landscapes, Still-lifes, and *Objets d'Art*)".

                    BERENSEN (V.O.)
          -- he summoned his uncles to the gallery
          on the *Esplanade des Charpentiers*.

INT. ART GALLERY. NIGHT

A showroom one flight up from the street. Summery landscapes on
one wall. Kitchen-table still-lifes on another. Bronze heads on
pedestals. Cadazio stands next to an easel which displays a
hidden artwork cloaked in velvet. He addresses his uncles Nick
and Joe.

                    CADAZIO
          We're done with flowers and fruit bowls.
          We're finished with beaches and
          seascapes. We're getting out of armor,
          rugs, and tapestries, too. I found
          something new. (In prison.)

Cadazio unveils the familiar canvas ("Simone, Naked, etc."). His
uncles immediately produce various corrective lenses
(spectacles, monocle, a magnifying glass) and stare for a long
moment. Finally:

                    UNCLE NICK
          Modern art?

                    CADAZIO
                    (profoundly)
          Modern art. Our specialty, starting now.

                    UNCLE JOE
                    (befuddled)
          I don't get it.

                    CADAZIO
                    (obviously)
          Of course, you don't.

                    UNCLE JOE
          Am I too old?

                    CADAZIO
                    (naturally)
          Of course, you are.

                    UNCLE NICK
                  (skeptical)
          Why is this good?

                    CADAZIO
                  (confident)
          It isn't good. Wrong idea.

                    UNCLE JOE
                  (bristling)
          That's no answer.

                    CADAZIO
                  (with satisfaction)
          My point. You see the girl in it?

                    UNCLE JOE/UNCLE NICK
                  (simultaneously)
          No.

                    CADAZIO
                  (definitively)
          Trust me, she's there.

As Cadazio goes to a cabinet of shallow file-drawers, opens the
top one, and withdraws a beige envelope, he continues:

                    CADAZIO
          One way to tell if a modern artist
          actually knows what he's doing is to get
          him to paint you a horse or a flower or a
          sinking battleship or something that's
          actually supposed to look like the thing
          it's actually supposed to look like. Can
          he do it? Look at this:

Cadazio opens the envelope and produces:

INSERT:

A charcoal drawing of a bird, simple and exquisite.

Uncle Nick holds the picture carefully by the edges and studies
it. Cadazio snaps his fingers.

                    CADAZIO
          Drawn in forty-five seconds right in
          front of me with a burnt matchstick.

                    UNCLE NICK
                  (now genuinely impressed)
          A perfect sparrow. That's excellent. May
          I keep it?

                    CADAZIO
          Don't be stupid. Of course, not. The
          point is: he could paint this --

After a brief, delicate tug-of-war, Uncle Nick, reluctantly,
releases the drawing back to Cadazio.

                    CADAZIO
          -- beautifully, if he wanted to, but he
          thinks this --

Cadazio points to "Simone".

                    CADAZIO
          -- is better.

Cadazio is almost surprised to realize that he, honestly, means
the following:

                    CADAZIO
          And I think I sort of agree with him.

The uncles examine the canvas, touching it, smelling it, etc.
Cadazio says with finality:

                    CADAZIO
          "Simone, Naked, Cell Block J. Hobby-room"
          is probably a masterpiece worth a
          significant, even exorbitant sum of money
          -- but not yet.

Uncle Nick folds his hands and nods. He says mystically:

                    UNCLE NICK
          The desire must be created.

Cadazio nods, also mystical. Silence. Uncle Joe blurts:

                    UNCLE JOE
          How long's he in for?

INT. HEARING CHAMBER. DAY

A court of law. Three magistrates on one side of an elevated
altar watch as Simone escorts Rosenthaler (in straitjacket and
leg-irons) from a side door to a central chair. She padlocks him
to the armrest. Rosenthaler sits, wary, facing his judges. Ten
rows of benches behind him are empty with the exception of the
front, occupied by Cadazio and his uncles. Simone, on a stool at
Rosenthaler's side, sets to work darning another child's sock as
the proceedings begin:

                    CHIEF MAGISTRATE
A new petition for special parole board
review has been filed on behalf of
Citizen 7524 in relation to the crimes of
Assault, Battery, and Violent
Dismemberment. Mr. Rosenthaler, why
should we put you back on the street?

                    ROSENTHALER
                 (softly)
Because it was an accident, your honor. I
didn't intend to kill anybody.

The Chief Magistrate raises an eyebrow. He says evenly:

                    CHIEF MAGISTRATE
You decapitated two bartenders with a
meat-saw.

Rosenthaler hesitates. He confers briefly with Simone at a
whisper. He nods and clarifies:

                    ROSENTHALER
The <u>first</u> bartender was an accident. The
second was self-defense.

The magistrates murmur. Simone resumes her darning.

                    CHIEF MAGISTRATE
Be that as it may: what demonstration of
genuine remorse or (at the very least)
regret can you offer? For beheading these
men.

Rosenthaler scratches his chin. He looks out the window. A bird
of prey snatches a white dove out of the sky in a puff of
feathers. Rosenthaler says, sincerely and genuinely apologetic,
almost inaudible:

                    ROSENTHALER
They had it coming.

                    CHIEF MAGISTRATE
                 (sharply)
I beg your pardon?

Cadazio interrupts loudly, more or less completely drowning out
Rosenthaler as he repeats himself:

       ROSENTHALER   CADAZIO
They had it coming?   Forgive me.

The Chief Magistrate frowns. Rosenthaler turns. Simone pauses
her darning. Cadazio, unexpectedly: has raised his hand.

                    CADAZIO
          Is there a part of this ritual where you
          ask if anybody has something to say
          before it's too late? Like at a wedding.

       CHIEF MAGISTRATE   CADAZIO
No.   I'll be brief.

Cadazio's uncles look uneasy but intrigued as Cadazio crawls
over a partition (slipping slightly as he struggles to get his
leg over) and "approaches the bench". The magistrates make no
effort to impede him -- though their expressions suggest extreme
disapproval. Cadazio launches into a persuasive spiel:

                    CADAZIO
          We all know this man is a murderer.
          Totally guilty of first-degree homicide,
          anyway you slice it. That's a given.
          However: he's, also, that rare, once-in-a-
          generation guy you hear about but never
          get the chance to discover for yourself:
          an artistic genius. Surely, there ought
          to be a double-standard for this sort of
          predicament. (Supposedly, he's a
          psychotic, by the way. That's not his
          fault.) Respectfully, I submit: maybe we
          could think up some other way to punish
          him? I'm looking for the wiggle-room.

Cadazio looks to his uncles. They nod, concerned and serious.
The magistrates are a stone wall.

                    BERENSEN (V.O.)
          Rosenthaler's right to petition for
          parole was permanently revoked for the
          duration of his sentence.

Simone is already putting away her darning. Uncle Joe interjects
from the stalls:

                    UNCLE JOE
          No further questions.

CUT TO:

Berensen at her lectern again.

                    BERENSEN
          Nevertheless, Cadazio and his uncles were
          unanimous in their decision to promote
          the artist as his exclusive brokers
          throughout the free world.

INSERT:

A promotional poster advertising a public debate in a town hall.
Across the top: a photograph of "Simone, Naked, etc." Across the
bottom: "The Next Mona Lisa?"

> BERENSEN (V.O.)
> "Simone" traveled far and wide.

MONTAGE:

The painting is shown on display in various exhibition spaces
around the world. In each location, a violent riot is in-
progress among art patrons in dinner jackets and evening gowns.
First: a municipal meeting hall in France. Champagne bottles fly
through the air, shattering and exploding.

> BERENSEN (V.O.)
> The Ennui *Salon*.

Next: a vast conservatory in England. Punching, choking,
shouting, screaming, bleeding.

> BERENSEN (V.O.)
> The Royal Exposition.

Finally: a tent at a middle-American harvest-festival with
carnival rides, cotton candy, shooting gallery, etc. One group
of attendees attempts to light the venue on fire while another
group resists them.

> BERENSEN (V.O.)
> The International Pavilion at the
> Liberty, Kansas State Fair (which was
> very nearly burned to the ground).

Cadazio and his uncles watch the destructive skirmish, eyes
bright, gleeful.

> BERENSEN (V.O.)
> In short, the picture was a sensation.

INT. AUCTION HOUSE. DAY

On the block: Rosenthaler's perfect sparrow. Paddles rise and
fall in rapid succession as an auctioneer, startled but
enthusiastic, tries to keep up with exuberant bidding.

> BERENSEN (V.O.)
> (Even the artist's all-but-forgotten,
> earlier work inspired wildly robust sales
> on the secondary market.)

Additional lots wait in the wings: Rosenthaler's previously-seen
still life, river view, flea-bitten dog, self-portrait, absinthe

bottle, and seated officer at desert fort (bullet hole still intact).

CUT TO:

Berensen at her lectern again.

> BERENSEN
> Meanwhile, Rosenthaler continued to work
> in confinement. Strikingly, the artist
> favored raw materials sourced exclusively
> from within the prison/asylum domain:

MONTAGE:

The camera shoots through an expansive pane of glass which fills the frame as Rosenthaler paints directly onto it, brushing and slashing in aggressive bursts (and jump-cuts), one color at a time. First: a dusty, pale orange.

> BERENSEN (V.O.)
> Powdered eggs.

Next: a thick, dark red.

> BERENSEN (V.O.)
> Pigeon blood.

Next: an oily black.

> BERENSEN (V.O.)
> Shackle grease.

Next: shades of dirty ash.

> BERENSEN (V.O.)
> Coal, cork, and dung.

Next: a waxy, nearly fluorescent, slightly sudsy yellow.

> BERENSEN (V.O.)
> Bright yellow scullery-soap.

Finally: a lukewarm porridge.

> BERENSEN (V.O.)
> And fresh cream of millet as a binding
> agent.

MONTAGE:

A naked Simone strikes various poses which appear to be (and, in fact, without the aid of visual effects, are) physically impossible. First: body twisted like a corkscrew, arms double-jointed akimbo, illuminated from a high window.

> BERENSEN (V.O.)
> Simone <u>liked</u> to stand still.

Next: flamingo-legged, fingers laced palms up, underlit by a flickering oil lamp.

> BERENSEN (V.O.)
> Indeed, she was Olympian in her ability
> to hold extremely challenging positions
> for extended periods of time.

Next: seated on a steaming radiator in thinker pose, puffs of breath visible in the frigid air.

> BERENSEN (V.O.)
> She exhibited very little vulnerability
> to extremes of heat or cold.

Next: in close-up, calmly ignoring a mosquito biting her cheek. It takes off, leaving only a tiny dot of blood which Simone wipes away with her pinky, perfectly clean.

> BERENSEN (V.O.)
> After even the most adverse forms of
> exposure, her skin remained unburned,
> unblemished, un-goose-pimpled.

Next: hanging upside down from a ceiling pipe in a frozen butterfly stroke.

> BERENSEN (V.O.)
> Another tidbit: she genuinely <u>enjoyed</u> the
> smell of turpentine --

Finally: cleaning splattered paint from her arms and legs with steel wool and distilled acid.

> BERENSEN (V.O.)
> -- and, in later years, actually <u>wore</u> it
> in the application of her toilet. (It's
> absolutely true. You could smell the
> solvent on her body.)

INT. EXECUTION THEATRE. DAY

A small, round chamber as tall as a silo. At a grated landing mounted to the wall: an open, iron clad hatch. The latch has been pried open, and the door handle lies below in a pile of splinters and screws. Narrow steps wind along the wall ten feet down to a disapproving guard with his hands in his pockets. He stands next to a control panel featuring a prominent throw-switch.

>   BERENSEN (V.O.)
>   She was more than a muse.

Rosenthaler says grimly, off-screen:

>   ROSENTHALER (O.S.)
>   Throw the switch.

The guard snorts dismissively. On the other side of the room: Rosenthaler is seated in an electric chair with a metal headband clamped around his forehead and leather bindings belted around his wrists. He explodes:

>   ROSENTHALER
>   Throw the switch, you cocksucker!

Simone appears in the doorway. She frowns.

>   SIMONE
>   What's wrong with you? Go back to work.

Rosenthaler looks slightly guilty -- but defiant. He insists:

>   ROSENTHALER
>   I can't. I won't. It's too hard. It's
>   torture. I'm -- I'm -- literally: I'm a
>   tortured artist.

Simone's eyes flash down to a half-finished bottle of mouthwash tucked discreetly next to one of the legs of the electric chair. She says gently:

>   SIMONE
>   Poor baby.

Simone descends the staircase as she says calmly to the guard:

>   SIMONE
>   Get out.

The guard exits. Simone stares at Rosenthaler, curious. Rosenthaler stares back at her, bitter. Simone reaches for the throw-switch and flips it for a fraction of a second. There is a powerful clack, and Rosenthaler takes a 10,000-volt zap to the body. His hair sparks, his body spasms, and smoke comes out of his ears. After a brief moment of frozen astonishment, trembling and smoldering, he glares at Simone, wary. Simone shrugs.

>   SIMONE
>   Is that what you want?

Silence. Simone approaches and stops in front of Rosenthaler
with her hands on her hips. She says, matter-of-fact:

>   SIMONE
>   I grew up on a farm. We didn't write
>   poetry. We didn't make music. We didn't
>   sculpt statues or paint pictures. I
>   learned arts and crafts technique from
>   books in this prison's library, and I
>   teach them as a volunteer. I don't know
>   what you know. I only know what you are.
>   I can see you're suffering. I can see
>   it's difficult. It might even get worse --
>   but then it's going to get better. You're
>   going to figure out whatever your problem
>   is. (What's your problem?)

>   ROSENTHALER
>   (crippled)
>   I don't know what to paint.

>   SIMONE
>   You're going to figure out what to paint,
>   and you're going to believe in yourself
>   (like I do), and you're going to struggle
>   -- and then, in the spring, or maybe the
>   summer, or possibly the fall, or, at the
>   very latest, the winter: this new work
>   will be complete. That's what's going to
>   happen.

Simone holds the throw-switch again -- Rosenthaler flinches --
as she asks:

>   SIMONE
>   Unless you still prefer to execute
>   yourself right now?

Rosenthaler slips his hands out the bindings and takes off the
metal headband, then ascends the steps and goes out the door.
Simone returns to the control panel and clicks off the power.
The electric chair jiggles and rattles as it hums down to
silence.

CUT TO:

Berensen at her lectern again.

>   BERENSEN
>   The French Splatter-school Action-group.

Berensen brings up a slide of a gathering of paint-splattered
men (burly, grumpy, unwashed, disheveled, stylish) and one woman
(small-boned but indestructible) posing for a photograph on the

street below a prison window. Rosenthaler, inside, smiles
broadly.

> BERENSEN
> A dynamic, talented, lusty, slovenly,
> alcoholic, violent pack of creative
> savages. They inspired and, often,
> personally attacked each other for two
> decades and more. (I'll have my drink
> now.)

Berensen reaches into a nook in the lectern and produces a small
thermos, which she empties, neat, into a short glass. She comes
out from behind her lectern and stands near the edge of the
stage, closer to the audience, sipping as she continues more
intimately:

> BERENSEN
> Remember, in those days, as you know, it
> was much more socially acceptable for a
> painter or sculptor to hit another fellow
> with a chair (or even a brick) or walk
> around with a black eye or a broken tooth
> and so on. Indeed, I'm jumping ahead,
> but, in my own experience, Rosenthaler
> could be quite unpredictably impulsive,
> meaning, I refer to the pigment-locker
> below his studio on the *Boulevard des
> Plombiers*, on one occasion, he grabbed me
> and put me in there, and, inappropri-
> ately, sort of, tried to --
>   (stage-whispering)
> -- fuck me against the wall in the corner
> of that pigment-locker. He <u>was</u> crazy
> (officially certified).

Berensen turns away and circles back behind her lectern. She
refers briefly to her notes, then presses on:

> BERENSEN
> The Cadazios, of course, represented them
> all.

EXT. COMPOUND ENTRANCE. DAY

Two guards slowly slide open a pair of high, steel-clad, spike-
topped, oak doors revealing Cadazio and his uncles waiting on
the road outside. In the reverse angle: two other guards slowly
slide open another pair of identical doors, revealing
Rosenthaler (shackles/straitjacket) waiting with Simone in the
recess court inside. The two opposing parties advance to meet at
a locked, iron-barred gate in the middle.

TITLE:

Three Years Later

Cadazio faces Rosenthaler, arms crossed, steely. Uncle Joe
stands behind him. A servant provides a chair for Uncle Nick who
sits with arms propped on the top of his cane. Cadazio addresses
Rosenthaler crisply:

> CADAZIO
> It's three years later. We've made you
> the most famous painter alive based on
> one small, scribbly, over-rated picture.
> You're an art school course. You're an
> encyclopedia entry. Even your disciples
> have won and squandered multiple
> fortunes. Yet you refuse to show us so
> much as a sketch or study for a single
> new piece during this entire, protracted
> period. How long are we meant to wait?
> Well, don't answer, because we're not
> asking. We already printed the
> invitations.

Uncle Joe holds up a letter-press card on thick, gold-trimmed
stock embossed luxuriously with scarlet script.

> CADAZIO
> We're coming in. All of us. The
> collectors. The critics. Even your second-
> rate imitators (we represent) who suck up
> to you and smuggle you goodies and
> probably turn out to be better than you
> are. The bribes, alone, are going to be
> outrageous, as these guards can assure
> you. But we're going to pay them. So
> finish it, whatever it is. The show's in
> two weeks.

Cadazio holds up two fingers. Rosenthaler grits his teeth,
stained and chipped. Once again, softly: he growls. (Another
guard, armed with a carbine, watches from a turret above.)
Cadazio retreats slightly while attempting to mask his
instinctive fear. He points to Simone:

> CADAZIO
> She thinks it's ready, by the way.

Rosenthaler flinches, surprised. He frowns and turns to Simone.
Simone nods.

> SIMONE
> It's ready.

Rosenthaler looks betrayed. Simone looks nonplussed. Cadazio
looks vindicated. Rosenthaler murmurs, vaguely optimistic:

                    ROSENTHALER
          I could use another year.

Cadazio screams in frustration, and his uncles throw their hands
up into the air, grip their hair, close their eyes, shake their
heads, etc.

CUT TO:

Berensen at her lectern again.

                    BERENSEN
          My employer, at that time, received the
          intriguing summons by rapid-priority
          wire. I refer, of course, to Upshur "Maw"
          Clampette.

Berensen brings up a triptych of black and white slides: one
shows a landmark, modernist residence resembling a doorstop
which overlooks a corn field; the other two show vitrines filled
with Ancient Greek, Roman, and Egyptian idols, tools, and
vessels.

                    BERENSEN
          Astute collector of antiquities.

Berensen remote-switches to another triptych: one shows a closer
view of the same house; the other two show rooms filled with
cubist and surrealist paintings and sculptures -- and the
visiting artists who created them.

                    BERENSEN
          Great friend to the *avant-garde*.

Berensen remote-switches to a slide of a pioneer-handsome, sixty-
year-old woman, slightly stout, perfect carriage, ebony black
eyes, dressed and done in the most highly refined,
sophisticated, continental style. She is outdoors, seated in an
armchair shaped like a lobster. She is Upshur "Maw" Clampette. A
water tower in the background reads: Liberty, KS.

                    BERENSEN
          Her collection, even in its infancy, was
          well-known and important (as was her
          residence, Ingo Steen's first American
          commission, known, informally, as the
          "Doorstop House"). It was my duty and, I
          may say, my privilege to catalogue,
          archive, and advise -- although she did
          whatever the hell she wanted no matter
          what you told her, anyway.

Berensen clicks off the projector.

                    BERENSEN
          Thus, we began the long journey from
          Liberty to Ennui.

EXT. SLEEPER PLANE. NIGHT

An amphibious aircraft in flight over the Atlantic Ocean (left
to right). Clouds wisp by in the background as we dissolve to a
cut-away view of the interior of the vessel. Waiters prepare
cocktails, and passengers read magazines. In first class,
privatized: Clampette (in an embroidered, kimono-style dressing
gown) sits at a low table smoking a cigarette and drinking a
night-cap as she completes her correspondence with the
assistance of a social secretary and a somewhat younger
Berensen, herself. Clampette rises, and a maid enters with an
ashtray and a hairnet which she stretches over her mistress'
head as they make their way down the aisle to a section of
curtained bunks. A doctor appears from aft with a tray of tonics
and remedies. He spoons two doses of milk of magnesia directly
into Clampette's mouth, followed by a brief hypodermic injection
to the shoulder. Berensen assists Clampette up the ladder to her
bunk and passes her a mystery novel open to the correct page.
Clampette offers Berensen her unfinished cigarette, and they
pass it back and forth, sharing the last few puffs before
Clampette pulls the curtains shut. Berensen enters the lower
bunk and pulls her own curtains shut. Her hand pokes out through
a gap in the fabric to tap ash onto the floor. The lights in the
cabin go dim.

Throughout this scene, Cadazio dictates in voiceover:

                    CADAZIO (V.O.)
          My dear Mrs. Clampette ("Maw", if I may),
          please, join us for the first-display of
          Mr. Moses Rosenthaler's extremely
          exciting new work (which I, myself, have
          not yet been permitted to see). In order
          to facilitate the viewing in a timely
          fashion, it may prove necessary for us to
          surreptitiously gain access to the
          facility where the artist currently
          resides. Please, rely on my operatives to
          organize any and all details and
          preparations for your visit. Caution: do
          not bring matches, lighters, or sharp
          objects of any kind. We await your
          confirmation with cheerful anticipation.
          Yours most truly, Cadazio Uncles and
          Nephew *Galerie* concern.

INT. ART GALLERY. NIGHT

Cadazio and his uncles wait, standing and seated in various
positions around the showroom. They are dressed for the evening.
Scarves and coats are draped on chair backs and pedestals. Three
thick bundles of large-format banknotes, each the size of a
sheet of writing paper, rest stacked on a gilded tabletop at the
center of the room. Each uncle checks the time (by pocket-watch,
wristwatch, or hourglass) while Berensen explains:

> BERENSEN (V.O.)
> The paddy-wagon collected us directly
> after the night's final round of working
> girls and revelers were delivered to the
> drunk-tank at 3am.

Cadazio opens the curtains to check the clock tower above the
place across the river.

CUT TO:

A high-angle shot racing up one of the city's narrow streets
following a motorcade composed of two police motorcycles and a
large paddy-wagon with cherry-lights whirling and sirens
howling, blasting, blaring, and wailing.

MONTAGE:

The rear section of a prisoner-transport vehicle with wire-mesh
windows and steel benches in two sets of tiered, facing rows.
The passengers include: Cadazio and his uncles; Clampette and
Berensen; Clampette's secretary; sixteen additional well-heeled
art collectors in furs, jewels, dinner jackets, black tie, etc;
the entire coterie of the French Splatter-school, as seen in the
earlier photograph, along with their girlfriends (who appear to
be prostitutes); and two, uniformed wait-staff. All carry copies
of an exhibition-program labeled Rosenthaler/Cadazio.

Overhead angle: Cadazio's hands count out a bribe into the palm
of the paddy-wagon driver.

A long, subterranean corridor of stone and mortar construction
with a narrow, brick path running alongside a coursing drainage-
gutter. Cadazio leads the procession described above, flanked
like a priest by two waterworks-men in pin-striped overalls (who
carry glowing acetylene gas-lamps) and the two wait-staff (who
push rolling hotel service-trollies).

Overhead angle: Cadazio's hands count out a bribe into the palms
of the two waterworks-men.

A cement-paved exercise yard seen from a high tower.
Searchlights, periodically, sweep across the walls and cast

barbed-wire shadows. The visitors traverse, diagonal, in silent single-file, escorted by a quartet of prison guards.

Overhead angle: Cadazio's hands count out bribes into the palms of the four guards.

A wide passage segmented by consecutive, iron-barred gates. Jeers and taunts echo and reverberate from rows of cells as the congregation advances behind a dozen prison guards *en masse* through the dimly-lit penitentiary.

Overhead angle: Cadazio's hands count out bribes into the palms of the twelve guards.

INT. RECREATION ROOM. NIGHT

An open doorway looking out from a pitch black space. The last guests, one by one, cross the threshold. The door closes, locks, and latches. We are in complete darkness. Long silence. A hushed murmur. Cadazio's voice calls out:

>   CADAZIO
> Moses, are you here?

A beat. Then: Rosenthaler's voice grunts from somewhere across the room:

>   ROSENTHALER
>   Uh-huh.

>   CADAZIO
>   (nervous)
> Any words of introduction? Or, perhaps, a
> welcome to our wonderful guests, some of
> whom have traveled a great distance to
> come see your work, I hope? Or,
> alternatively, just, I don't know. Hello?

>   SIMONE
>   (also in the dark)
>   Lights.

There is a contact-bang, and the hobby-room (the previously-seen white-washed hall the size of a squash court) lights up bright: the space is now entirely muraled in ten astonishing panels, each sixteen feet tall, as seen in Berensen's lecture-slides. (Now, for the first time, we see them in color, and they are magnificent.)

Rosenthaler, seated in a wheelchair, wears a mattress-ticking necktie with his prison uniform. He is stone-faced. Simone stands at his side.

Cadazio absorbs the view: the artist and the opus. His mouth
falls open. His eyes goggle. He shouts at the silent gathering:

>   CADAZIO
>   Quiet, please!

A moment. Suddenly, Cadazio bubbles over and exclaims, voice
cracking and screeching like an adolescent schoolboy's:

>   CADAZIO
>   I did it!

Cadazio pumps his fists and scrabbles to the center of the room,
spinning in all directions to observe the encircling artwork.
His voice alternates between delirious hollering and reverential
whispering:

>   CADAZIO
>   It's good! This is historic. I did it.
>   Open the champagne!

Corks pop, and the wait-staff sweep through the mingling crowd
with trays of *coupes* and *canapés*. Cadazio approaches
Rosenthaler.

>   CADAZIO
>   Why are you sitting in a wheelchair like
>   an invalid? You should be dancing on the
>   tables! It's a triumph!

>   SIMONE
>   He stabbed himself in the thigh with a
>   palette knife last week, but, luckily,
>   the infirmary-boy was able to reconnect
>   the artery.

>   ROSENTHALER
>   (genuinely)
>   Do you like it?

>   CADAZIO
>   Do I like it?
>   (humbled)
>   Yes.

Cadazio leans down and kisses Rosenthaler on the forehead. He
turns to Simone and kisses her, as well. The entire group of
Splatter-school artists approaches. One of their companions
speaks to Rosenthaler on their behalf:

>   PROSTITUTE
>   They did your girlfriend for you.

Each artist holds up a small portrait: a drawing on a napkin, a sketch on the exhibition program, a sculpture made from a champagne cork and its wire-cage, etc. Rosenthaler bows and mumbles thank-you's, moved and embarrassed (though not very impressed). Cadazio points:

> CADAZIO
> Look at "Maw". She's mesmerized.

Across the room, Clampette stands close to one of the panels, mesmerized, indeed. Berensen lingers some distance behind her. Cadazio approaches briskly and idles at her side. Clampette says, eventually, in the twang of her region:

> CLAMPETTE
> This here's a fresco, t'weren't it?

> CADAZIO
> (dazzled)
> Precisely! He's a Renaissance master of the highest order! He mines the same vein as Piperno Pierluigi when he illuminated the Christ before God's heavenly altar in 1565! "Maw"! Nobody has an eye for things nobody has ever seen like "Maw" Clampette of Liberty, Kansas! We should be ashamed to even gather in her presence! Why the fuck did she say fresco?
> (shouting at Rosenthaler)
> Are they painted into the walls?

Cadazio reaches out to touch the picture. He rubs it more forcefully. He scratches and claws at it with the fingernails of both hands, grimacing in panic. He is thunder-struck.

> CADAZIO
> Oh, no. What has he done? You fucking asshole.
> (desperately to Berensen)
> Look at this.

> BERENSEN
> I think it's utterly wonderful.

> CADAZIO
> It's crucial! It's probably a turning point in the evolution of human pictography! Scratched and plastered into a reinforced cement aggregate gymnasium! He even painted on the radiators!

> CLAMPETTE
> (speculating)
> Maybe one of them resterashun fellers out
> (more)

> CLAMPETTE (cont'd)
> at the *Fondazione dell'Arte Classico*
> could figger a way to rustle them
> pitchers loose.

> CADAZIO
> We're in a maximum-security prison,
> "Maw"! It's federal property! Even to
> <u>begin</u> the bureaucratic nightmare would
> require years of negotiation with a team
> of highly-paid, arrogant, obnoxious
> advocates. I don't even know how you'd
> peel them off. It's a fresco.

Cadazio, abruptly, darts away and sails across the room to
confront Rosenthaler. He detonates:

> CADAZIO
> It's a fresco!

> ROSENTHALER
> (puzzled)
> So what?

> CADAZIO
> Can you even begin to fathom the shit-ton
> of money my uncles and I have squandered
> to get to this point-of-no-return? Look
> at them!

Cadazio points. His uncles watch and listen. They do not appear
to comprehend the situation on any level.

> CADAZIO
> You've ruined us! Does that mean nothing
> to you?

> ROSENTHALER
> (injured)
> I thought you liked it.

> CADAZIO
> (ruthlessly)
> I think it <u>stinks</u>. Get out of that
> wheelchair! I'm going to kick your ass up
> and down this hobby-room!

Rosenthaler tenses and winces as if he has been, literally,
stabbed in the back. He growls (as before).

> CADAZIO
> Don't growl at me, you convicted
> murderer. You homicidal, suicidal,
> psychopathic, no-talent drunk!

Without rising, Rosenthaler charges Cadazio like a rolling
rhinoceros, torquing his wheels with powerful force, kicking and
lunging as Cadazio dodges and feints. Cadazio throws champagne
into Rosenthaler's eyes, blinding him briefly, then darts behind
the hulking artist and grabs the handles of his wheelchair. He
shoves hard and sprint-pushes Rosenthaler, rumbling across the
open gallery, launching the wheelchair and its passenger at
speed directly off a three-step ledge. The wheelchair is
airborne for an instant, then lands, skidding, with a thunk, and
continues at high velocity directly into the cement center of
one of the vast panels. It smashes with a cracking, metallic
thud. The room goes dead silent. Rosenthaler is immobile.

Simone turns to Cadazio, stern. Cadazio looks sheepish.

Suddenly, Rosenthaler quick-reverses, spins around, and
accelerates, bumpily rocketing back up the steps (with
remarkable athleticism) and re-charging Cadazio like an even
more ferocious rolling rhinoceros. Cadazio flees. The assembled
guests watch, surprised, perplexed, amused, frightened, side-
stepping as: the two combatants circle the perimeter of the
room, screaming at each other furiously. As they whiz by Simone,
she deftly extends her foot, tripping Cadazio into a tumbling
spill, and, in almost the same instant, flips the hand-brake
lever on the wheelchair, freezing the axles and obliterating the
spokes. The vehicle, essentially, disintegrates as Rosenthaler
ejects through space, landing heavily directly on top of his
representative.

Cadazio, flat on his back, speaks up into Rosenthaler's face:

                    CADAZIO
          Get off me, Moses.

The fight is over. Rosenthaler, hobbling, is assisted to a
stool, onto which he crumples and wilts. Cadazio asks Simone,
bewildered:

                    CADAZIO
          Why didn't you tell me, *gardienne*?

Simone thinks for a minute. She starts to explain, then
simplifies it:

                    SIMONE
          Because you would've stopped him.

Cadazio deflates. He nods. He retreats among his uncles, who
appear to be woozy and disoriented. Uncle Nick fans himself with
an exhibition-program. Uncle Joe takes a tablet from a tin and
washes it down with champagne. Cadazio says, heartbroken:

                    CADAZIO
We have to accept it. His need to fail is
more powerful than our strongest desires
to help him succeed. I give up. He's
defeated us. It's sad, but there it is.
Anyway, at least, he finished the mother-
fucker.
          (philosophical)
It is, perhaps, the most interesting
contemplation of peripheral vision I've
ever seen.

Cadazio shields his vision with his flat palm and pivots side to
side, studying the work out of the corners of his eyes. As he
returns to Rosenthaler, Rosenthaler throws open his arms, and
the men embrace like two exhausted prizefighters. Tears stream
down their faces.

                    CADAZIO
Well done, Moses. This has a greatness to
it. If you plastered it deep enough, it
may last. We'll come see it again one
day. God willing. You'll, already, still
be here, of course.

Rosenthaler shrugs. He says softly:

                    ROSENTHALER
It's all Simone.

They watch Simone, on the opposite side of the room, standing
with her back to them, centered in front of another of the
massive panels. Berensen informs us (from the future):

                    BERENSEN (V.O.)
At that moment, they were both aware of
Simone's intention to leave her position
at the Ennui Prison/Asylum the following
day, endowed with funds provided by the
Cadazios as compensation for her work as
Rosenthaler's model and muse.

Cadazio puts his hand on Rosenthaler's shoulder.

                    BERENSEN (V.O.)
She was re-united with the estranged
child to whom she had given birth in her
youth, and the two never again lived
apart.

Simone turns around to look at Rosenthaler and Cadazio. She
smiles and imitates the pose -- albeit cubist -- implied in the
painting: a runner at full stride, diving across an imaginary
finish line. (Her balance, of course, is impossibly perfect.)

                    BERENSEN (V.O.)
          She and Rosenthaler maintained a regular
          correspondence for the rest of the
          artist's life.

In the meantime: Clampette and Berensen carefully study the
surfaces of one of the other panels. Berensen wears archivist's
white cotton gloves as she assesses the qualities of the
material.

                    BERENSEN
          It's certainly an extremely challenging
          task. The medium appears to be grease and
          blood deep-permeated into a grain-based,
          seamless gesso. I think you'd have to
          take it <u>whole</u>.

                    CLAMPETTE
                (optimistic)
          I reckon that rascal Maurizio might fry
          up a s'looshin in his noggin. He's a
          crafty, old sidewinder.

                    BERENSEN
                (taking a note in her agenda-book)
          I'll contact him early tomorrow morning,
          "Maw".

Simone sits perched on the knee of Rosenthaler's good leg,
darning another child's sock (of a somewhat larger size than
previously-seen). Berensen glides over to Cadazio.

                    BERENSEN
          Mrs. Clampette would like to put the
          piece on hold.

Cadazio's face goes blank and frozen. He mutters, stunned:

                    CADAZIO
          The half-sticker?

                    BERENSEN
          Yes, please. Should she choose to
          finalize the sale: will this amount be
          acceptable to you and your uncles?

Berensen hands Cadazio a slip of paper. He whisks on a pair of
reading glasses. His uncles materialize to huddle around,
peering over his shoulder. They murmur their approval. Cadazio
asks Berensen:

                    CADAZIO
          Can we get a deposit?

                    BERENSEN
              (calling out to Clampette)
        "Maw"? An advance against the total sum?

                    CLAMPETTE
        Tell them stingy Frenchmen I ain't making
        no promises.

Cadazio and his uncles appear to be, tentatively, relieved.
Uncle Nick signals to the band. The music resumes, and the party
revives.

                    BERENSEN (V.O.)
        "Ten Reinforced Cement Aggregate (Load-
        bearing) Murals" was to remain on hold
        under the name Upshur Clampette for the
        subsequent twenty years.

One of the wait-staff, hovering nearby, interjects
confidentially:

                    WAIT-STAFF
        Mr. Cadazio? The prisoners are asking to
        be bribed, as well.

Cadazio hesitates. He asks, irritated:

                    CADAZIO
        Which prisoners?

                    WAIT-STAFF
        All of them. There's an angry mob outside
        the hobby-room. This individual claims to
        be their representative.

The wait-staff points to a wiry, scrappy, gristly, previously-
unseen convict loitering at his side. Cadazio does a double-take
and frowns. He says sharply, eye-balling the convict:

                    CADAZIO
        Tell them we don't bribe rapists and pick-
        pockets. It's unethical. Besides, I
        didn't bring an additional six million
        francs in small bills.

Cadazio strides to the door and pokes his head out. In the
corridor, there is, indeed, an angry mob of approximately 300
prisoners holding improvised weapons (broom handles, pipe-
sections, bricks and chains). Cadazio asks them rhetorically:

                    CADAZIO
        How'd you get out there?

Cadazio leans back inside and shouts to Rosenthaler:

                    CADAZIO
          What do we do?

                    ROSENTHALER
                    (grimly)
          Lock the door.

Cadazio attempts to re-slam the door, but the convict resists
and grapples with him. Simone baton-whomps him on the top of his
head with all her might. Blood spurts as the convict yelps and
bellows in a thundering baritone:

                    CONVICT
          Riot!

Iron hinges shoot off in three directions as if blasted apart by
explosive charges, and the hobby-room door whangs flat onto the
floor with a boom. The mob stampedes into the art exhibition:
berserk, blood-thirsty, and spectacularly out of control. The
assembled guests, screaming and scrambling, attempt to defend
themselves.

                    BERENSEN (V.O.)
          In the aftermath, 72 prisoners and six
          members of the French Splatter-school lay
          dead or mortally wounded.

Simone continues to baton-whomp numerous convicts. Cadazio
smashes a champagne bottle and jabs it into the faces of various
attackers. Clampette produces a Derringer pistol, shoots two men
dead, and reloads. Berensen discharges a high-pressure fire
extinguisher into the melee. The artists and their prostitutes
fight like sailors. Cadazio's uncles struggle to prevent
themselves from being strangled to death.

                    BERENSEN (V.O.)
          Moses Rosenthaler, for acts of extreme
          valor which saved the lives of nine
          guards, twenty-two distinguished
          visitors, and the Ministers of Culture
          and Urbanity, received his freedom (with
          probation for life) --

For the first time in the evening, Rosenthaler unsteadily rises
to his feet. In one hand: a large can of red paint (pigeon
blood). In the other: a bottle of turpentine. Again: he growls.

                    BERENSEN (V.O.)
          -- and was decorated in the Order of the
          Caged Lion.

Close-up: Rosenthaler swigs the turpentine, throws the bottle
aside, pours the full can of paint over the top of his head,

lights a match, and roars, berserk (splattering: people, painting, and camera). He spits, breathing fire.

EXT. CARGO PLANE. DAY

A military aircraft in flight over the Atlantic Ocean (right to left). Clouds wisp by in the background as we dissolve to a cut-away view of the interior of the vessel. In the massive rear-cabin: an army tank, a troop carrier, three jeeps, and the entire hobby-room, intact, suspended from the ceiling trusses on a net-cradle. It sways slightly in the mild turbulence.

> BERENSEN (V.O.)
> One score later, as per "Maw" Clampette's
> detailed instructions, Cadazio and his
> own nephew arranged for the entirety of
> the hobby-room to be relocated onboard a
> Goliath Aviation twelve-engine artillery
> transport directly from Ennui to Liberty.

Side by side in jump-seats with four-point harnesses and parachute backpacks: a gently aging Cadazio and his bright, eager, young relation.

CUT TO:

The hobby-room. Berensen and the audience from her lecture have gathered inside the transplanted structure to view Rosenthaler's creation. Outside the open doorway: a corn field rustles in the prairie breeze.

> BERENSEN (V.O.)
> In this form, the *avant-garde* assumed its
> place upon the plains of Central Kansas.

INT. WRITER'S OFFICE (BERENSEN). DAY

At the window: Berensen studies slides and re-orders them in a carousel tray. In the corner: the accountant makes notations on slips and tickets. In the middle of the room: Howitzer paces, shuffling a sheaf of receipts, muttering/quoting under his breath:

> HOWITZER
> "Pencils, pens, erasers, thumbtacks,
> pushpins, typewriter repairman..."

Howitzer interrupts himself, looking over his glasses at Berensen:

> HOWITZER
> Why am I paying for a hotel room at a
> beach club on the North Atlantic coast?

                    BERENSEN
               (slightly offended)
          Because I had to go there to write it.

Howitzer grumbles, unconvinced. He shuffles more receipts and
resumes his muttering/quoting:

                    HOWITZER
          "Breakfast, lunch, dinner, laundry,
          nightcap, midnight snack..."

Howitzer interrupts himself (looking over his glasses) again:

                    HOWITZER
          What's wrong with the desk right here? In
          your office, courtesy of this magazine.

                    BERENSEN
               (slightly more offended)
          Don't ask me to be indiscreet. About what
          happened between me and Moses at a
          seaside inn twenty years ago. We were
          lovers. I went back to remember.

                    HOWITZER
               (pause)
          On my dime.

                    BERENSEN
               (firmly)
          Yes, please.

Howitzer grumbles once more. He says to the accountant,
resigned:

                    HOWITZER
          Add it up.

The accountant totals the figures on her adding machine.

Story #2
(pages 59 to 96)

INSERT:

The proof-print of a correspondent's diary in the
Politics/Poetry Section. A line-drawing depicts a Citroën
economy-car, vandalized and on fire.

TITLE:

> Youth Movement
> "Revisions to a Manifesto"
> by Lucinda Krementz

INT. DEAN'S OFFICE. NIGHT

A paneled room of generous proportions with high ceilings and a
vast, ancient table at its center. Seated across from each
other, cross-legged, in the middle of the desktop: a middle-aged
professor (tall, distinguished, rigid) and a nineteen-year-old
boy (skinny, wild-haired, electric). They both stare intently
at, situated between them: a chessboard. The professor keeps his
fingers on a bishop while he re-thinks. The boy (Zeffirelli)
puffs on a dark, skinny, Tuscan cigar. The room overflows all
around with a hundred students and a dozen faculty, standing on
cabinets, sitting on floors, crouched on windowsills, spilling
into the corridors and vestibules. All stare at the two players,
mid-match.

A voice (American, chain-smoker, low [for a woman]) begins:

> KREMENTZ (V.O.)
> March first. Negotiations between
> undergraduates and the university
> administration break down abruptly in
> early-morning hours after clamorous
> debate, angry name-calling, and, finally,
> outright gambling over: the right of free-
> access to the girls dormitory for all
> male students.

In the corner: two boys (a giraffe and a fire-hydrant) whisper
simultaneously. They are Vittel and Mitch-mitch.

VITTEL	MITCH-MITCH
Zeffirelli's cramping the professor's bishop.	He should open the position and counter with both rooks.

At the chessboard, the professor releases his bishop and taps a
game clock. Zeffirelli makes a brisk move, knight to bishop etc,
and taps the timer himself.

> KREMENTZ (V.O.)
> The protest (which ended in a stalemate)
> gave the superficial appearance of a
> vanity exercise for the pimple-cream and
> (more)

                    KREMENTZ (V.O.) (cont'd)
          wet-dream contingent; but, in fact, the
          sexes were equally represented, and all
          participants emphasized the basis of
          their frustration: a desire (more: a
          biological need) for freedom, full-stop.

Discreetly seated on the top shelf of a bookcase in a corner, a
sensible, fifty-year-old woman (skirt-suit, pearls, trench coat,
large handbag) watches, listens, smokes a cigarette, and takes
notes in a composition book. She is deeply curious, deeply
engaged, entertained/amused. She is Lucinda Krementz. She
frowns, then yells:

                    KREMENTZ
          Young lady: shoes!

Across the room: a student in a turtleneck sweater, uniform
smock, long socks with sandals, and checker-striped motorcycle
helmet (worn at all times throughout the story) is standing on
the hem of a tapestry (knights, ladies, lions, unicorn) while
she checks her make-up in a powder-puff compact mirror. She
looks down at her feet, mortified. She carefully steps off the
draped cloth and neatens it. She looks back to Krementz and
sticks out her tongue. She is Juliette. Krementz raises an
eyebrow. At the table: the professor thwarts an attack on the
queen's flank. Various quarters of the room cheer and grumble.

                    KREMENTZ (V.O.)
          It has exploded into symbolism, and
          everybody's talking about it.

INT. DINING ROOM. NIGHT

A comfortable fifth-floor flat cluttered with books and papers.
Seated at a futuristic, white, round table over a spotless,
white, round rug: a forty-ish couple. The husband wears a
pullover sweater and long sideburns. The wife wears a caftan and
long braids. In the background: twin girls, thirteen, eat alone
in the kitchen, listening to a news report on the radio.
Krementz faces her friends, chilly, as the husband twists a
corkscrew.

                    KREMENTZ (V.O.)
          March fifth. Late supper at the B's.
          Eldest boy, nineteen, not home since
          yesterday morning. Father chanced upon
          him, mid-day, marching alongside his
          comrades. Their slogan:

CUT TO:

A stone wall. Spray-paint graffitied onto it: *"Les Enfants sont
Grognons."*

                    KREMENTZ (V.O.)
            "The children are grumpy."

CUT TO:

Krementz lighting a cigarette as the wine is poured. She says,
matter-of-fact:

                    KREMENTZ
            I'll be needing an ashtray, if you care
            about this carpet.

The husband moves briskly to fetch a receptacle. The wife,
sheepish, sits in silence. Krementz looks up coolly at a not-
entirely-successful chandelier.

                    KREMENTZ (V.O.)
            Local news reports: fascist law students,
            loitering at the university gates with
            intent to harass left-wing demonstrators
            (their natural enemies), instead, brawl
            in their defense when police forces move
            to break up the demonstration.

The husband delivers an oversized, crystal bowl (which appears
to weigh about ten pounds) and clunks it onto the table under
Krementz's cigarette just as ashes begin to crumble.

                    KREMENTZ
            Thank you.

Krementz exhales a stream of smoke as the husband slides back
into his seat, uneasy.

                    KREMENTZ (V.O.)
            An additional dinner guest, thus far,
            fails to appear. For this, I am grateful.
            (Had not been informed of his invitation,
            in first place.)

The husband and wife respond simultaneously, finishing each
other's sentences:

            HUSBAND   WIFE
We didn't mean to offend you.   We thought you might decline
We're sorry.   the invitation. If we warned
                                 you.

                    KREMENTZ
            You were right.

Faintly, outside: shouting, chanting, a periodic ricochet-pop.

                    KREMENTZ (V.O.)
        Medical student on Radio-Ennui describes
        aggressive crowd-control methods in use
        on street today. Quote:

            WIFE   HUSBAND
Just give him a chance. He's   How long's it been? Since
very intelligent.   what's-his-name?

                    KREMENTZ
                    (patient)
        I know you mean well.

                    KREMENTZ (V.O.)
        "It begins with a prickly tingling of the
        exposed skin."

Strangely: Krementz and the couple -- all three, at once --
reach not for their wine but, instead, glasses of water. They
each drink a quick, solid gulp. As soon as Krementz swallows:

                    KREMENTZ
        I'm not an old maid.

            HUSBAND   WIFE
We don't think that.   Of course, you're not.

                    KREMENTZ (V.O.)
        "Then: a reddening and swelling of the
        orbital muscles."

All three begin to blink, squint, and sniffle.

                    KREMENTZ
        Take me at my word: I live by myself on
        purpose. I prefer relationships that end.
        I deliberately choose to have neither
        husband nor children (the two greatest
        deterrents to any woman's attempt to live
        by and for writing). Why are we crying?

            HUSBAND   WIFE
Because it's sad. We don't   Loneliness is a kind of
want you to be alone.   poverty.

                    KREMENTZ
        I'm not sad. My eyes hurt. There's
        something wrong with your apartment.

Pause. At the same instant: Krementz and her hosts begin to
cough, choke, and rub their eyes. The noise in the streets has
now erupted into a rumbling, clattering roar, punctuated by
megaphone shouts and a mixture of sirens.

                        KREMENTZ (V.O.)
          "Finally: a barrage of searing pain as
          snot pours from the nostrils, and the
          throat spasms and constricts."

                HUSBAND   WIFE
Spread a damp cloth on every   I can't believe it reaches us
windowsill.   up here. On the fifth floor.

The husband stands up and moves toward the curtains as a bright
light flashes outside. Distant thumps reverberate. The wife goes
into the kitchen to sweep the girls down the back corridor.
Krementz puts a napkin to her face and drifts across the
apartment, into a bathroom. She closes the door.

INT. BATHROOM. NIGHT

White tiles, dangling towels, a family of toothbrushes. Krementz
glares at herself in the mirror. Her eyes are blood-shot. Her
mascara is smudged. She turns on the tap and watches the water
run. Behind her: a subtle splash. She frowns. A pair of bare
feet balanced on the rim of the end of the tub shift and wiggle.
Krementz crosses the room and whisks the shower curtain fully
open with a jingling tug. Zeffirelli, soaking, turbaned in
terrycloth, smoking another skinny cigar, looks shocked. He
holds a graph-paper notebook and a four-color ballpoint pen
poised mid-sentence. Pause.

                        ZEFFIRELLI
          I'm naked, Mrs. Krementz.

                        KREMENTZ
          I can see that.

                        ZEFFIRELLI
          Why are you crying?

                        KREMENTZ
          Tear gas.

Zeffirelli sniffs the air. Krementz quietly realizes and/or
acknowledges:

                        KREMENTZ
          Also, I suppose I'm sad.

Zeffirelli nods, thoughtful. He and Krementz lock eyes for a
moment.

                        ZEFFIRELLI
          Please, turn away. I feel shy about my
          new muscles.

Krementz jerks the shower curtain shut again. She goes back to
the sink, searches in the medicine cabinet, and finds a tube of
mascara. She fixes her eyes.

                    KREMENTZ
          Go tell your parents you're home. They're
          worried.

                    ZEFFIRELLI (O.S.)
          I'm expected back on the barricades.

                    KREMENTZ
               (skeptical)
          I didn't see any barricades.

                    ZEFFIRELLI (O.S.)
               (hedging)
          Well, we're still constructing them.

                    KREMENTZ
               (evenly)
          Uh-huh. What are you writing?

Zeffirelli slings the shower curtain open again. He holds up his
notebook and says vigorously:

                    ZEFFIRELLI
          Our manifesto. I told them not to invite
          Paul, by the way. Maybe you're sad, but
          you don't seem lonely to me.

                    KREMENTZ
               (vindicated)
          Exactly!

                    ZEFFIRELLI
          I saw you at the protest. On top of a
          bookcase (taking notes).
               (tantalized)
          Is there a story in us? For the people of
          Kansas.

                    KREMENTZ
               (pause)
          Maybe.

                    ZEFFIRELLI
               (re: his manifesto)
          Then you should study our resolutions.
          Or, anyway, will you proofread it? My
          parents think you're a good writer.

                    KREMENTZ
          Give it to me.

Zeffirelli jolts up out of the tub, splashing and naked, lunges across the bathroom, thrusts the graph-paper notebook into Krementz's hands, then darts away and slips back into the water. Krementz opens the notebook and reads, frowning, flipping pages. Outside the room: a doorbell rings, a dog barks. Krementz says, skeptical:

>   KREMENTZ
>   It's a little damp.

>   ZEFFIRELLI
>   (hesitates)
>   Physically? Or metaphorically.

>   KREMENTZ
>   Both. Based on the cover --
>   (water-stained)
>   -- and the first four sentences.

>   ZEFFIRELLI
>   (offended)
>   Don't criticize my manifesto.

>   KREMENTZ
>   (raising an eyebrow)
>   Oh. You don't want remarks?

>   ZEFFIRELLI
>   (less certain)
>   I don't _need_ remarks. Do I? I only asked
>   you to proofread it because I thought
>   you'd be even more impressed by how good
>   it already is.

>   KREMENTZ
>   Let's start with the typos.

>   ZEFFIRELLI
>   (squinting)
>   What's there?

Krementz produces a red felt-tip pen and immediately begins grading the document like a book report. Zeffirelli watches tensely.

CUT TO:

Krementz emerging with the graph-paper notebook in hand. A tall, wispy-bearded, blond man in corduroy waits, seated, with the couple at the table. He immediately rises to his feet. It is clear: the journey from wherever he has come from has been difficult. His sleeve is ripped. His shirt is torn. There is a small bandage on his forehead. He is dusty, mussed, and bruised. He smiles, reserved. He is Paul. Krementz nods:

                    KREMENTZ
Hi.

          HUSBAND   WIFE
Paul Duval.   Lucinda Krementz.

                      PAUL
                (bowing slightly)
          How do you do?

Krementz stiffens as Paul kisses her on both cheeks.

                    KREMENTZ
          Your beard is scratching me.

Paul withdraws slightly. Krementz tucks herself back into the
group. Paul sits, then holds forth at some length while Krementz
continues in voiceover:

                    KREMENTZ (V.O.)
          Unexpected guest finally arrives. Looks
          like hell. Describes odyssey across city:
          stalled trains, stalled buses, broken
          windows, paving stones flying in all
          directions.

The girls, back in the kitchen, now in pajamas with the shirts
pulled up over their noses, raise the volume on the radio. The
husband refills glasses. The wife passes around a bowl of
radishes. Paul, in the meantime, summarizes:

                      PAUL
          Can the faculty succeed if the students
          fail? It remains to be seen. Anyway:
                (changing gears)
          Here we are. The famous Lucinda. Hello.

Paul smiles. Krementz says bluntly, signaling "stop":

                    KREMENTZ
          I didn't know you were coming. They
          didn't tell me. This is not an official
          meeting.

Paul hesitates. He looks to the husband and wife. They murmur,
uneasy. Krementz suddenly clutches her pearls, rolls back her
eyes, makes a gurgling sound, mock-suffocating, then plunks her
face down on a plate and plays dead. Paul opens his mouth and
pauses. The husband looks up at the ceiling. The wife looks down
at the table. The bathroom door opens again, and Zeffirelli
enters. He now wears a transparent rain slicker over his clothes
and a gas-mask over his face. His voice echoes inside the
breathing-device:

                    ZEFFIRELLI
          Good evening.

The husband and wife are, momentarily, speechless. Zeffirelli
offers a second gas-mask to Krementz. She stands up, puts it on,
and reverbs to her hosts:

                    KREMENTZ
          Start without me.

Krementz follows Zeffirelli out through the *salon*. Off-screen:
the apartment's front door opens and shuts. Paul, puzzled, and
the couple, angry/humiliated/worried, remain at the table in
uneasy silence. The girls, watching from the kitchen, snicker
under their pajama shirts.

INT. WALK-UP APARTMENT. DAY

A narrow bedroom on a high floor. Krementz (in a rose *peignoir*)
sits up in bed eating burnt toast, reading from her composition
book, and rapid-transcribing on a portable typewriter balanced
across her knees. Zeffirelli, beside her on the mattress, naked
(as usual), flips manifesto-pages, bristling at the numerous,
red correction-marks. She smokes a cigarette, he smokes another
skinny cigar.

                    KREMENTZ (V.O.)
          March tenth.

Zeffirelli does a double-take. He points across the room and
says false-modestly:

                    ZEFFIRELLI
          Me, again.

Krementz looks up.

INSERT:

A small, black and white television set on a rolling cart at the
foot of the bed. On screen: an anchorman delivers a bulletin,
then introduces footage -- subtitled: "Last Night" -- of a
battalion of riot-police (billy-clubs and plastic shields)
facing off against a legion of student protesters (paving stones
and broken bottles). On a plastic crate in the small space
between the two transfixed, opposing groups: another chessboard.
In a sudden burst of attack/counter-attack, Zeffirelli and a
riot-police commander trade pawns, bishops, rooks, etc. then
pause. (A superimposed chessboard diagram re-caps the moves that
lead up to this caesura.)

                    KREMENTZ (V.O.)
          City services at a halt, one week and
          counting. Public transportation:
               (more)

                    KREMENTZ (V.O.) (cont'd)
          suspended. Piles of garbage: uncollected.
          Schools on strike. No mail, no milk.

Zeffirelli moves his queen diagonally seven spaces to capture
the queen of his rival. The collected military personnel and
young radicals gasp in unison, grimace, groan, and whisper
nervously. (A flashbulb pops.) Zeffirelli says discreetly:

                    ZEFFIRELLI
          Check.

The riot-police commander, unfazed, protects his king with an
unforeseen, defensive side-step. Zeffirelli, surprised, nods
with guarded admiration. (A super-title blinks: "Stalemate!")

                    KREMENTZ (V.O.)
          What will normal reality be? Next week,
          next month, whenever (if ever) we get the
          chance to experience it again. Anyone's
          guess. Impossible to imagine these
          students (exhilarated, naive, brave in
          the extreme) returning to their obedient
          classrooms.

Krementz looks to Zeffirelli. He has resumed bristling over her
corrections. He points:

                    ZEFFIRELLI
          What's this part?

Krementz leans over and squints to study the page.

                    KREMENTZ
          I added an appendix.

                    ZEFFIRELLI
               (in disbelief)
          You're joking.

                    KREMENTZ
               (innocent)
          No, I'm not.

                    ZEFFIRELLI
               (appalled)
          You finished my manifesto? Without me.

                    KREMENTZ
          I made it sound like you, I think. Just
          more clear, more concise, a bit less
          poetic. Put it this way: this isn't the
          first manifesto I've proofread.

Zeffirelli is insulted. The doorbell rings. Krementz gets out of
bed, leaves the room, and closes the door behind her. Muffled
voices echo through the wall/door. Zeffirelli frowns, anxious.
He strains to eavesdrop. He bites a fingernail. Krementz comes
back in and returns to the bed. Zeffirelli stares at her,
waiting. Finally:

                    ZEFFIRELLI
          Who was that?

                    KREMENTZ
          Your mother.

                    ZEFFIRELLI
                (agitated)
          My mother? What'd she want? Did you tell
          her I was here?

                    KREMENTZ
          Yes.

                    ZEFFIRELLI
                (stunned)
          Why?

                    KREMENTZ
                (simply)
          Because she asked. I don't lie.

                    ZEFFIRELLI
                (worried)
          Was she upset?

                    KREMENTZ
          I don't think so.

                    ZEFFIRELLI
                (doubtful)
          What'd she say?

                    KREMENTZ
          She nodded.

                    ZEFFIRELLI
                (hesitates)
          What'd you say?

                    KREMENTZ
          I told her I was working on an article
          about you and your friends.

                    ZEFFIRELLI
                (intrigued)
          So you are.

                    KREMENTZ
                  (shrugs)
        I've already written a thousand words. I
        asked to interview her.

                    ZEFFIRELLI
                  (disoriented)
        Did she agree?

                    KREMENTZ
        Of course.

                    ZEFFIRELLI
                  (very agitated)
        Well, I am upset. I don't know how to
        feel. Am I in trouble? Why would my
        mother be so calm? Is it proper? This is
        all off the record. Everything. My whole
        life.
                  (vulnerable)
        What am I supposed to do now?

                    KREMENTZ
                  (pause)
        I should maintain journalistic
        neutrality.

Long pause. Zeffirelli says genuinely (perhaps growing up ever
so slightly in this moment):

                    ZEFFIRELLI
        I like how ruthless you are. It's part of
        your beauty, I think. You've got a
        thousand words already?

Krementz nods, flattered, and points at the page in her
typewriter. Zeffirelli peers at it. Krementz covers it with her
hand. Zeffirelli returns to his manifesto. Krementz types one
more short paragraph.

                    KREMENTZ (V.O.)
        The kids did this. Obliterated a thousand
        years of republican authority in less
        than a fortnight. How and why? Before it
        began: where did it begin?

INT. STUDENT CAFÉ. NIGHT

The front room of the *Sans Blague* bubbles over with
caffeinated/inebriated twenty-year-olds chattering shoulder to
shoulder along counters, booths, and banquettes. Classical music
blasts on the jukebox. A crowd hovers over a pinball machine
decorated with question marks, infinity symbols, atoms/molecules
and the caption: "Modern Physics!" A waiter speed-navigates

through the circus with a rattling tray triple-tiered with
double-espressos extended high above his head.

(Note: each young patron of the café carries a highbrow/semi-
unreadable paperback of some variety at all times without
exception.)

TITLE:

                    Last Spring

Zeffirelli assumes the narration:

                    ZEFFIRELLI (V.O.)
          It was another time, it was another
          Ennui. Must be nearly six months ago, I
          guess. (My sisters were still twelve,
          anyway.)

INSERT:

An illuminated jukebox title-strip labeled G-7: "Dansez le
'Craze'". Zeffirelli continues in voiceover:

                    ZEFFIRELLI (V.O.)
          You danced the Craze and the *Lait Chaud*.

MONTAGE:

A hiss, a scratch, then the first note of a French pop-
instrumental (an uptempo, beepy/jingly fugue). The camera
dollies among undergraduates with brush-cuts, mop-tops,
pageboys, and frizzy perms. The boys wear topcoats, two button
tweeds, and skinny high-waters. The girls wear knitted mini-
dresses, ballet flats, and leotards.

                    ZEFFIRELLI (V.O.)
          You wore your hair-do in the Pompidou,
          the Crouton, or the *Fruits-de-Mer*.

A standing foursome of boys and girls talk simultaneously in
gibberish. One makes a symbolic hand shape followed by a
wiggling gesture. The others laugh.

                    ZEFFIRELLI (V.O.)
          Your slang mixed bits of Latin with
          philosophy jargon and manual signaling.

A balustraded, low-ceilinged mezzanine-loge at the top of a
spiral staircase. The *menu du jour* specials on the wall-
chalkboard have been rubbed out and carefully vandalized into:
"French Tongue on Shit Sandwich." Juliette (seen earlier
standing on the tapestry in the dean's office) sits at a table

checking her make-up in her compact mirror as she addresses a
pack of admirers/detractors.

> ZEFFIRELLI (V.O.)
> Devil's advocates bickered and debated
> perpetually, *ad nauseum,* only for the
> sake of argument:

> JULIETTE
> I couldn't disagree more.

Pairs of opposing cliques go head to head at backgammon, Risk,
and crossword puzzles; vie at competitive domino toppling
(winding/climbing/fanning arrangements which click-clack their
way through the café doing tricks with matchsticks, shoelaces,
and sparkling water); and -- here we see Zeffirelli, Vittel, and
Mitch-mitch each at a separate board/game -- play chess.

> ZEFFIRELLI (V.O.)
> Every clique had a rival. The Nuts had
> the Bolts. The Sticks had the Stones. The
> Jocks had <u>us</u>: the Bookworms --

Mitch-mitch, listless and distracted, re-reads a well-creased
letter, then moves a pawn and taps the game-clock timer. His
opponent immediately takes the piece. Pause.

> ZEFFIRELLI (V.O.)
> -- until Mitch-mitch failed the
> baccalaureate and got sent down to
> National Duty Obligation (three months in
> the Mustard Region).

Mitch-mitch tips over his king, crumples his letter, pulls on
his topcoat, and leaves the table. He re-enters frame outside
the plate-glass window (late afternoon, drizzle), lighting a
cigarette as he jogs through criss-crossing traffic before
descending into the Flop Quarter Métro station.

Zeffirelli watches from his chessboard, concerned. He looks to
Vittel. Vittel shrugs. Zeffirelli snatches up the crumpled paper
from Mitch-mitch's table and unfolds it.

INSERT:

An official summons red-stamped on flimsy, blue card-stock.
Across the top: Report for Compulsory Martial Chores.

CUT TO:

Night. Two tables frown at each other from corners of the front-
room. Juliette checks her make-up in her compact mirror.

TITLE:

One Month Later

                JULIETTE
Where were his principles when he agreed
to fight on behalf of an imperialist army
in an unjust war of totalitarian
aggression?

                ZEFFIRELLI
          (in disbelief)
He got sent to the Mustard Region. For
National Duty-obligation.

                VITTEL
It's required.

                JULIETTE
          (confident)
It's the same.

                ZEFFIRELLI
How dare you? Who gave you permission to
besmirch our friend? Does it occur to
you: he's very probably marching in the
middle of the night right now carrying a
fifty-pound sack of gun-powder and
peeling stale potatoes while he digs a
latrine trench in the rain with a tin
cup? He doesn't want to be in the
military.

                VITTEL
It's required!

                JULIETTE
He should burn the patch and desert his
post.

A general gasp: conversation in the rest of the café has fallen
silent, and everyone is listening to the Mitch-mitch debate. A
whispered aside from a pre-law student at another table:

                SMART GIRL
Minimum punishment: six-months sentence
and a Black Mark in permanent ink.

Zeffirelli, recovering from the affront, snaps back at Juliette:

                ZEFFIRELLI
That's easy for you to say. From the
comfort of the *Sans Blague*.

                    JULIETTE
                   (confident)
          It's the same.

A new voice interrupts off-screen:

                    MITCH-MITCH (O.S.)
          For once: she's right.

Everyone turns. Mitch-mitch is standing alone in the open doorway at the end of the crowded bar, in front of the crowded
terrasse. He is dressed in a long, blue, floor-length cape, a
navy beret, and blue commando trousers tucked into muddy combat-
boots. He carries an enormous blue-camo duffel-sack over his
shoulder. The eyes of every customer are now glued to him.
Zeffirelli stammers then finds his tongue:

                    ZEFFIRELLI
          Mitch-mitch, what are you doing here?
          You're supposed to be in the Mustard
          Region for another two months.

In close-up: Mitch-mitch is a wounded soldier (psychologically).
Krementz returns in voiceover with the following information:

                    KREMENTZ (V.O.)
          Five years later, I, myself, translated
          Mitch-mitch Simca's poetic interpretation
          of his National Duty Obligation service
          (the flashback scene in Act II of
          "Goodbye, Zeffirelli").

INT. CADET BARRACKS. NIGHT

A cement-box garrison dormitory dimly lit from the flies. Three-
tiered bunkbeds delineate the upstage backdrop (cinder block and
timber joist). Downstage, left: an industrial drum-heater idles,
bubbling. Downstage, right: a five seat latrine with noisy
pipes. A single, bare lightbulb hangs, suspended, above
centerstage.

On cots and footlockers: eighteen cadets in white boxer shorts,
tucked-in white undershirts, and shower slippers. A drill-
sergeant, dressed in the same garments with the addition of a
white kepi and gun-belt, leans on a bunk ladder, sipping from a
plastic mess-kit teacup. He speaks at a stage-whisper to the
rapt troop:

                    DRILL-SERGEANT
          In North Africa, I caught a bullet in the
          tail; in South America, I caught a chunk
          of high-explosives shrapnel in the left
          wing; in East Asia, I picked up a rare,
          microbial, infectious gut-parasite in the
                     (more)

                    DRILL-SERGEANT (cont'd)
          lower abdominal cavity -- and I've got
          them all with me right now, still in my
          body: but I don't regret my choice to
          wear this uniform --

The drill-sergeant motions across his costume (as indicated, his
skivvies).

                    DRILL-SERGEANT
          -- and, in sixteen years, I'll get my
          pension.
                    (checks watch)
          Well, that's your bedtime story, ladies.
          Lights out!

The cadets scramble to their bunks, shouting a ritual of call-
and-response/nighttime orders ("Hup! Ho! Hut!" "Lights out!
Blankets on!" "Covers tucked! Eyes shut! Pray your prayers!"),
followed by a general murmur of grateful, holy, reverential,
hushed muttering, signs-of-crossings, and "Amens" -- then
silence. (The drill-sergeant ascends a spiral staircase and
retires to an upstairs desk and cot seen only in silhouette
against a glowing, white rectangle.)

A top-bunk cadet rustles under his sheets.

                    CADET #1
          Psst.

Long pause. The top-bunk cadet rustles again and props himself
up on an elbow.

                    CADET #1
          Psst. Mitch-mitch. Psst.

Pause, again. The top-bunk cadet sits up fully.

                    CADET #1
          Psst. Mitch-mitch. What do you want to
          be?

Mitch-mitch (portrayed in this scene by a theatre-actor with
well-trained "instrument"), one bunk-tier below, leans out,
reluctant/annoyed.

                    MITCH-MITCH
          What?

                    CADET #1
          What do you want to be, Mitch-mitch?

Mitch-mitch sighs. As he answers, resigned, the rest of the
cadets creep out of their cots and return to their earlier
positions, listening.

                    MITCH-MITCH
With my grades? I'll be an assistant-
pharmacist.

                    CADET #2
Will that make you be satisfied?

                    MITCH-MITCH
                (evenly)
It won't depress me. I should've studied
harder.

                    CADET #1
And you, Robouchon?

                    CADET #3
I have no choice. I'll work for my
father's glass factory. Someone has to
take over.

                    CADET #1
It's normal.

                    CADET #2
Vaugirard. What's your plan?

                    CADET #4
I suppose, I'll continue to be an
attractive wastrel, like my cousins on
both sides of the family.

        CADET #1   CADET #3
Your cousins are the best.   I love your cousins.

                    MITCH-MITCH
                (pause)
What about you, Morisot?

No answer. Mitch-mitch repeats the question:

                    MITCH-MITCH
Morisot? What do you want to be?

Morisot, bespectacled, timid, pale, answers softly from the
bottom bunk:

                    MORISOT
A protester.

                    CADET #1
                (hesitates)
What'd he say?

                    CADET #2
          He said, "A protester."

                    CADET #3
                  (puzzled)
          What does he mean?

                    CADET #1
          I don't know.

                    CADET #4
                  (doubtful)
          I thought Morisot was going to be a
          professor of geological chemistry.

Mitch-mitch cranes upside-down to examine Morisot. He says,
surprised:

                    MITCH-MITCH
          Morisot's crying.

A voice in the darkness, across the room, hushes sharply:

                    VOICE
          Shhh!

Cadet #1 bolts up on his knees. He shout-whispers, angry:

                    CADET #1
          Who said, "Shhh!"

Silence. Morisot speaks again, quiet but determined:

                    MORISOT
          I won't do it.

                    MITCH-MITCH
                  (uncertain)
          It's only eight more weeks, Morisot.
          Before we complete the program.

                    MORISOT
          I don't mean the program. I mean from
          when we go home until retirement age.
          That 48-year period of my life, I mean.
          That's what I won't do. I can no longer
          envision myself as a grown-up man in our
          parents' world.

Morisot slides open the window next to his cot, and discreetly
slips out into the night. A beat, then a sickening thud. Mitch-
mitch gasps, astonished, and shouts:

                    MITCH-MITCH
          Morisot!

Mitch-mitch drops and tucks into Morisot's bunk. He screams,
pained:

                    MITCH-MITCH
          He went out the window!

Other cadets scramble to join Mitch-mitch as he sticks his head
out and looks down.

                    CADET #1
          Is he dead?

                    MITCH-MITCH
          I don't know.

                    CADET #2
          How far did he fall?

                    MITCH-MITCH
          Five floors with high ceilings.

                    CADET #3
          It rained last night. Maybe the mud's
          still soft.

                    MITCH-MITCH
          He's not moving.

The stage-lights begin to slowly, slowly dim as Mitch-mitch's
voice, diminishing in volume, softer and softer, repeats:

                    MITCH-MITCH
          He's still not moving.
               (pause)
          He's still not moving.
               (pause)
          He's still not moving.
               (pause)
          He's still not moving.
               (pause)
          He's still not moving.

CUT TO:

The café, exactly as we left it. Mitch-mitch crosses the silent
room to join his friends. Zeffirelli, confused and moved, stands
up and kisses Mitch-mitch on both cheeks. Mitch-mitch embraces
Zeffirelli. He turns to face the larger group. He steps up onto
a chair and points to a tricolor patch on his chest the shape of
a shield which depicts a flying bullet and the words: Mustard
Region Cadets. He says simply:

                    MITCH-MITCH
          I can no longer salute this patch.

Mitch-mitch rips off the patch and ignites it with a Zippo. The
room (including Juliette) gasps again. Zeffirelli, stunned,
mouth open, begins to slowly clap. Juliette joins him. Vittel
claps faster. A wave of thunderous applause spreads through the
room.

                    ZEFFIRELLI (V.O.)
          The next morning Mitch-mitch was arrested
          for Desertion and Desecration, and the
          Sans Blague became headquarters for the
          Movement of Young Idealists for the
          Revolutionary Overthrow of Reactionary
          Neo-liberal Society.

Above the jukebox: Juliette pulls down a glossy headshot of a
heartthrob (blue eyes, bronze skin, golden hair) taped to a
mirrored-wall and starts to replace it with a glossy headshot of
a public intellectual (round spectacles, woolen scarf, pipe).
Zeffirelli, edgy, pops up at her side:

                    ZEFFIRELLI
          What are you doing?

                    JULIETTE
          Replacing Tip-top with François-Marie
          Charvet.

                    ZEFFIRELLI
               (stupefied)
          They can live together. Tip-top with
          Charvet.

                    JULIETTE
          Tip-top is a commodity represented by a
          record company owned by a conglomerate
          controlled by a bank subsidized by a
          bureaucracy sustaining the puppet-
          leadership of a satellite stooge-
          government. For every note he sings, a
          peasant must die in West Africa.

Zeffirelli, stony, drops in a twenty-centime coin and punches
two buttons. Another hit French single (high-tenor vocals and
expansive, orchestral backing) gusts into the room. Spinning
lights circle. Immediately: the café is dancing -- and, at the
chorus, singing, *fortissimo*, in unison with "Tip-top".

Zeffirelli and Juliette stare at each other coolly, then drift
apart into their respective crowds. Krementz resumes the role of
narrator:

                    KREMENTZ (V.O.)
          There followed: a brisk, unpredictable
          tit-for-tat between Ennui's elders and
          its youngers.

From one corner: Juliette watches Zeffirelli reflected in her
compact mirror. From the opposite: Zeffirelli studies Juliette
in a reflection of a reflection of an angled ceiling-mirror. He
puffs on his skinny cigar.

MONTAGE:

The *cour* of a dilapidated residential hotel. A thick-set
gardienne framed in the upper-section of a Dutch door gossips
darkly with an amiable *gendarme* and a group of elderly,
intrigued neighbors (eye-doctor sunglasses, mesh grocery-sacks).

                    KREMENTZ (V.O.)
          August. Community whisper-campaign
          denounces student movement.

An *impasse* alongside the *Sans Blague*. A squad of disorderly
police-goons dumps barrels of coffee beans into a sewer-canal.

                    KREMENTZ (V.O.)
          September. *Sans Blague* coffee-license
          revoked by official decree.

A mansard platform on a tall building above the *quai*. Vittel and
two other headphoned student disc-jockeys with cigarettes in
their mouths speed-talk at a microphone inside a tiny,
ramshackle transmission booth next to a jerry-rigged
broadcasting tower twenty feet high.

                    KREMENTZ (V.O.)
          October. Propaganda Committee erects
          pirate-radio tower on Physics Department
          rooftop.

A long, formica-top table in a kitchen with tiled walls and
hanging copper pots and pans. Two dozen grandparents, aunts,
uncles, and cousins eat slices of an enormous, thin *galette* the
size of a bicycle wheel. Mitch-mitch, in pajamas, wears a paper
gold-foil crown on his head.

                    KREMENTZ (V.O.)
          November. Mitch-mitch released to
          parental custody.

An idle librarian staring into space. Behind her: rows and
aisles of shelves, stacks, racks, carts -- all completely empty
and desolate.

> KREMENTZ (V.O.)
> December. Check-out Protest at the
> *Bibliotèque Principale* (entire library
> circulation legally removed until five
> minutes before incur of massive overdue-
> book fines).

The steps of the university lunchroom. A line of students, arms-
linked, lunch-trays brandished like shields, obstructs a bank of
entrance-doors.

> KREMENTZ (V.O.)
> January. Meal-plan Blockade of the
> undergraduate cafeteria.

The facade of a student-housing *pension*. Female students in
crowded windows lower improvised ropes down to male students
hanging from the ledges below.

> KREMENTZ (V.O.)
> February. The Girls Dormitory Uprising.
> It all, in the end, leads to --

EXT. WIDE BOULEVARD. EVENING

One half-block of a paving-stone avenue between and below facing
banks of imposing, cut-stone apartment buildings. On one end: a
barricade of school-desks, chairs, bookcases, globes,
microscopes, and typewriters piled fifteen feet high. On the
other end: compact cars, burned black, still smoldering, on
their sides, upside-down, standing on end, split in two, etc. On
opposing flanks: two cafés, the *Fleurs du Mal* and the *Americain*.
A thread of gutter-water runs down the center of the road like a
stream through a canyon. Métro station: Bootblack District.

> KREMENTZ (V.O.)
> -- March: the Chessboard Revolution.

Student protestors sit in clusters on the piled rubble and
mutilated cars; crouch on and dangle from storefront awnings and
ledges; direct traffic (one of them, anyway). Innocent
bystanders (old and young) stand on balconies and in open
windows; wait on tables and eat/drink at the *terrasses* of the
two cafés; pose for a tourist-family picture (T-shirt: "Liberty
Junior High Boys Track"). A platoon of riot-police stands in
formation beyond the barricade, fifty meters down the street.
Mitch-mitch and Vittel occupy the middle of the improvised
barrier -- near Juliette, who sits perched alone on the top of a
folding ladder. Each (protesters, bystanders, riot-police) holds
a pale pink pamphlet with *"Le Sans Blague: a Manifesto"* sloganed
across its letter-pressed cover. They all read intently,
periodically turning pages.

Zeffirelli, anxious, lingers among his comrades, attending their reactions (especially Juliette's). He fidgets with his skinny cigar. A voice booms over a loudspeaker:

> RIOT POLICE (O.S.)
> *Le petit roque!*

Zeffirelli, Mitch-mitch, and Vittel dart away to a metal cart with a chessboard on it (black pieces only). Zeffirelli sits down on a cane-backed dining room chair. He studies his options for a fraction of a second, then moves a knight against his invisible opponent. Mitch-mitch quickly writes in chalk on a small slate and thrusts it up into the sky on a long, skinny pole.

CUT TO:

The riot-police. A communications signaler at the spearhead sits at his own metal cart operating a remote field-telephone system. He raises a pair of binoculars to his eyes.

INSERT:

The binoculars' P.O.V. The slate peeking over the top of the school-desk barricade reads: "Kt. to Q.B.3".

The signaler relays a message into his handset receiver:

> SIGNALER
> Knight to queen's bishop three.

CUT TO:

The situation room at the Ennui *Mairie* (long conference table, tall leather chairs, numerous television sets). A cabinet aide listening on the other end of the telephone line nods and scribbles on an official memo-pad. He presents the message to: the mayor (seventy-five, white moustache, rolled up shirtsleeves/unbuttoned waistcoat), seated at his own chessboard (white pieces only), surrounded by a team of political advisors and game-strategy analysts.

> CABINET AIDE
> Mr. Mayor? He moved.

The mayor studies the message briefly (counsel peering over his shoulders), then flicks it aside and looks at the board, hands on hips. He puts his fingers to his own knight, pauses while his team murmurs support/uncertainty, then makes an assertive move.

CUT TO:

The riot police. The signaler nods and shouts the capture into a microphone, blasting from the loudspeaker:

                         SIGNALER
              Le cavalier prend le cavalier!

CUT TO:

Zeffirelli. He removes his knight from the board, folds his
hands, and concentrates. Mitch-mitch and Vittel resume reading
the pink pamphlet. Zeffirelli, distracted, asks:

                         ZEFFIRELLI
              What page you on?

Mitch-mitch and Vittel answer simultaneously, eyes glued to
pages:

              VITTEL   MITCH-MITCH
Final chapter.   Last paragraph.

Zeffirelli waits. (The sun sets. Street lights blink on.) Mitch-
mitch and Vittel close their pamphlets and nod slowly with
intrigued admiration, deeply thoughtful. Just as they begin to
speak: Juliette's voice barks sharply from the top of her
ladder:

                         JULIETTE
              You call this a manifesto?

Zeffirelli, Mitch-mitch, and Vittel look up. Juliette descends
to the ground, fuming.

              VITTEL   MITCH-MITCH
Don't you?   What's wrong with it?

                         ZEFFIRELLI
                         (defensive)
              I think so. By definition.

Other student protesters begin to gather around. Juliette opens
to a marked page and shouts:

                         JULIETTE
              Page two, "Proclamation 7".

Members of the growing audience open their pink pamphlets and
quickly turn to the indicated paragraph. Juliette runs her
finger along the text, rapid-muttering unintelligibly to herself
under her breath until she arrives at the pertinent passage --
which she then declaims with angry, emphatic, bitter contempt.
Krementz, in voiceover, drowns her out:

                         KREMENTZ (V.O.)
              In spite of the purity of their cause (to
              create a free, borderless, utopian
              civilization), the students, nevertheless,
                         (more)

                              KREMENTZ (V.O.) (cont'd)
                    split into factions before fully uniting
                    in first place.

Juliette flips to another marked passage.

                              JULIETTE
                    Page five, "Edict 1(b)".

Juliette rapid-mutters, then declaims again under Krementz's:

                              KREMENTZ (V.O.)
                    One thing is now finally clear: they are
                    answering their parents. What do they
                    want? To defend their illusions. A
                    luminous abstraction.

Juliette flips to another marked passage.

                              JULIETTE
                    Page eleven, "Appendix Roman numeral
                    III".

Juliette rapid mutters/declaims a third time. Krementz:

                              KREMENTZ (V.O.)
                    I am convinced they are better than we
                    were.

Juliette, having finished her quotations, now holds up the
pamphlet, outraged, and gives her critique:

                              JULIETTE
                    Who approved the unauthorized allocation
                    of funds for the mass-printing of this
                    obtuse, ambiguous, poetic (in a bad way)
                    document? I'm the treasurer, supposedly!
                              (pointing to vestigial organ)
                    And who needs an appendix, anyway?

Mitch-mitch and Vittel, unswayed, comment admiringly to
Zeffirelli:

          MITCH-MITCH   VITTEL
That's the best section of the   My favorite part, maybe.
whole pamphlet.

                              ZEFFIRELLI
                         (hesitates)
                    Mrs. Krementz suggested it, actually. The
                    appendix.

                              JULIETTE
                         (overhearing)
                    Mrs. Krementz wrote it?

                    ZEFFIRELLI
                   (correction)
          Polished it. Certain passages.

The assembled group now turns to, previously unseen, just
outside the inner circle: Krementz, taking notes in her
composition book. She looks slightly sheepish. Juliette objects:

                    JULIETTE
          Why is she participating? She should
          maintain journalistic neutrality.

Mitch-mitch and Vittel respond immediately and simultaneously:

          VITTEL   MITCH-MITCH
No such thing. Doesn't exist.   Journalistic neutrality is a
                                 discredited concept.

Juliette, disgusted, rips her copy of the manifesto to shreds.
Zeffirelli is horrified.

                    JULIETTE
          We didn't appoint you (or Mrs. Krementz)
          spokesman for us. Your job is to play
          chess.

Zeffirelli points at the scraps on the ground. He explains:

                    ZEFFIRELLI
          I inscribed it to you.

                    JULIETTE
                   (hesitates)
          Oh.

Juliette crouches down and digs among the bits of paper. She
finds one with a handwritten dedication on it. She reads it,
then tucks it into her shirt pocket.

                    JULIETTE
          I'll save this souvenir, but for the rest
          of it: I couldn't disagree more.

Juliette checks her make-up in her compact mirror. Zeffirelli
looks wounded. Mitch-mitch and Vittel pat him on the back.
Krementz, eye-balling Juliette in disapproval, says in
voiceover:

                    KREMENTZ (V.O.)
          Remind myself: you are a guest at this
          manifestation. Not my fight. Stay out of
          it, Lucinda. Keep your mouth shut.

Nevertheless, Krementz interrupts herself out loud:

                    KREMENTZ
          I have to say something.
                    (to Juliette)
          You're a very bright girl, Juliette. If
          you'd put away your powder-puff (for one
          minute, forgive me) and think for
          yourself (for one minute, forgive me) you
          might realize: you're all in this
          together. Even the riot-police.

Juliette pauses, frozen in her mirror. The crowd of student
protesters, eager and intrigued, draws closer, gossiping at a
whisper. Juliette snaps her compact shut and says,
confrontational but respectful:

                    JULIETTE
          I'm not a child, Mrs. Krementz. I always
          think for myself.
                    (including her comrades)
          We all do.

Mitch-mitch and Vittel respond simultaneously again:

          MITCH-MITCH   VITTEL
I wouldn't say that.   Some do. Some don't.

The signaler's voice booms over the loudspeaker again:

                    SIGNALER (O.S.)
          À vous!

                    ZEFFIRELLI
                    (tense)
          Our move.

                    JULIETTE
                    (to Mrs. Krementz)
          You believe I haven't informed myself
          properly? Or taken important matters
          seriously? I assure you, it's not the
          case.

                    KREMENTZ
                    (backpedaling)
          That was impolite. Of me. I withdraw the
          remark.

Zeffirelli looks back and forth between Krementz and Juliette.
Long pause (more whispered gossip). Juliette shrugs,
indifferent:

                    JULIETTE
          If you wish.

                    KREMENTZ
                 (honestly)
        I beg your pardon.

                    JULIETTE
                 (detached)
        Very well.

                    KREMENTZ
                 (sincerely)
        I'm sorry.

                    JULIETTE
                 (coldly)
        Noted.

                    KREMENTZ
                 (hardening)
        Thank you. You're sure?

                    JULIETTE
        Of course.

Juliette turns away to go -- then (on second thought) returns,
suspicious:

                    JULIETTE
        Sure about what?

                    KREMENTZ
                 (matter-of-fact)
        Sure you're not a child.

                    JULIETTE
                 (stiffening again)
        Quite sure.

                    KREMENTZ
                 (bluntly)
        Then learn to accept an apology. That's
        important.

Juliette's eyes darken. Aside, the pre-law student announces in
a hushed voice:

                    SMART GIRL
        It's a fight! The old American versus the
        revolutionary, French teenager.

Juliette, derisive, demands:

                    JULIETTE
        Important to whom?

                    KREMENTZ
                 (frankly)
         Grown-ups.

The signaler booms over the loudspeaker again once more:

                    SIGNALER (O.S.)
              À vous!

                    ZEFFIRELLI
                 (frustrated)
         Our move. The mayor's waiting.

Juliette, exceedingly flustered, blurts harshly:

                    JULIETTE
         I don't object to you sleeping with him,
         Mrs. Krementz. We all have that freedom.
         (It's a fundamental human right we fight
         for, in fact.) What I object to is:
                 (slightly hysterical)
         I think you're in love with Zeffirelli!
         That's wrong; or, at the very least, it's
         vulgar. You're an old maid.

The entire avenue (miraculously) goes dead silent. Krementz has
the full attention of every protester and bystander in the
vicinity. She blushes bright red. In an instant: her eyes fill
with fierce tears. She says quietly, dignified:

                    KREMENTZ
         Kindly leave me my dignity.

Zeffirelli explains rapid-fire, firmly, gently to the group:

                    ZEFFIRELLI
         She's not an old maid.
                 (to Juliette:)
         She's not in love with me.
                 (to the group:)
         She's our friend.
                 (to Juliette of Krementz:)
         I'm her friend.
                 (to Krementz of Juliette:)
         She's confused.
                 (to Juliette of Krementz:)
         She wants to help us.
                 (to Krementz of Juliette:)
         She's angry.
                 (to the group:)
         She's a very good writer.

Zeffirelli turns to Krementz. Krementz bows, accepting the
compliment. Zeffirelli asks, concerned:

                    ZEFFIRELLI
          It's a lonely life, isn't it?

Krementz stares at Zeffirelli, surprised. She hesitates. She
looks to Juliette. Juliette's lips part, but she does not speak.
Krementz says softly:

                    KREMENTZ
          Sometimes.

CUT TO:

The situation room. The cabinet aide, holding the telephone
receiver, says to the mayor at his chessboard:

                    CABINET AIDE
          Still no response.

The mayor frowns. He picks up a game clock and looks at the
timer. He shrugs.

                    MAYOR
          Rubber bullets and tear gas.

CUT TO:

Krementz in close-up, eyes still filled with tears:

                    KREMENTZ
          It's true. I should maintain journalistic
          neutrality. If it exists.

CUT TO:

Juliette in close-up, now crying, as well:

                    JULIETTE
          Please, excuse me, Mrs. Krementz.

Krementz takes Juliette's hand and clutches it briefly. She nods
and smiles. Juliette looks upset and uncomfortable. Zeffirelli,
beside and between them, is powerless, puzzled, and moved. A
volley of tear-gas canisters, flash grenades, and sound bombs
flies through the air behind the trio, bursting, blazing,
banging, sparking, popping, etc. Protesters scatter away in all
directions. Krementz dismisses the display with a reassuring:

                    KREMENTZ
          It's just fireworks.

Zeffirelli and Juliette, slightly awed, remain in place with
Krementz. The phalanx of riot-police surges over and around the
barricade, flooding the street, swinging clubs, firing rubber
bullets, deflecting paving stones and flying bottles, etc.

Ignoring the entire commotion, Krementz points at Juliette and
says to Zeffirelli:

                    KREMENTZ
          She's the best of them.
               (then, to both)
          Stop bickering. Go make love.

Zeffirelli and Juliette grimace, embarrassed. Krementz points
at, nearby, a checker-striped (matching Juliette's helmet)
motorcycle leaning on its kickstand. Zeffirelli and Juliette
turn to look at each other. Juliette says openly:

                    JULIETTE
          I'm a virgin.

                    ZEFFIRELLI
               (hesitates)
          Me, too -- except for Mrs. Krementz.

Pause. Krementz says politely, with a shrug:

                    KREMENTZ
          I thought so.

Automatically, in unison, Zeffirelli and Juliette jump on the
motorcycle. He wraps his arms around her waist. She produces the
ignition key from her pocket, inserts/twists it, kicks the
starter, and guns the engine. One of the student protesters
rolls aside a mesh-steel bin filled with gym equipment
revealing: a gap in the barricade. Mitch-mitch and Vittel
scramble through, followed by a dozen of their shouting comrades
-- and Juliette (with her passenger) on the motorcycle. They
shoot away, up the avenue.

Krementz stands alone at the center of the commotion.

                    KREMENTZ (V.O.)
          March fifteenth.

INSERT:

A desktop, a coffee cup, an ashtray. Krementz's hands snap open
her composition book -- revealing, in the process, a glimpsed,
unexpected stray entry (in four colors of ball-point pen) upside-
down on the last page. She immediately flips back and rotates
the journal to study it.

                    KREMENTZ (V.O.)
          Discover on flyleaf of my composition
          book: a hasty paragraph.

EXT. WALK-UP APARTMENT. NIGHT

The facade of an old building of modest flats. The camera zooms
out from Krementz reading/smoking, lamp-lit in her bedroom
window, to reveal the windows of her neighbors (cooking,
ironing, vacuuming, glued to television sets and radios).

>   KREMENTZ (V.O.)
>   Not sure when Zeffirelli had the chance
>   to write it. Late that night, while I
>   slept? Poetic (not necessarily in a bad
>   way). Reads as follows:

CUT TO:

The motorcycle racing down a wide, eerily vacant boulevard.
Zeffirelli's voice:

>   ZEFFIRELLI (V.O.)
>   Postscript to a Burst Appendix: an
>   invincible comet speeds on its guided arc
>   toward the outer reaches of the galaxy in
>   cosmic space-time. What _was_ our cause?

SPLIT-SCREEN:

A pair of slow-motion portraits (eyes directly into camera). On
the left, Krementz, body wrapped in a damp towel, hair pinned
and netted, pearls; on the right, Juliette, shirtless in a
brassiere, face smeared with cold cream, plastic shower cap.
They stare at themselves in the mirror.

>   ZEFFIRELLI (V.O.)
>   Recollection of two memories. You: soap-
>   scent of drugstore shampoo, ashtray of
>   stale cigarettes, burnt toast. Her:
>   perfume of cheap gasoline, coffee on the
>   breath (too much sugar), cocoa-butter
>   skin. (Where does she spend her summers?)
>   They say it's the smells you finally
>   don't forget. The brain works that way.

CUT TO:

The motorcycle, another angle. Zeffirelli, clutching Juliette,
closes his eyes. Smoke and embers swirl from his skinny cigar.

>   ZEFFIRELLI (V.O.)
>   (I've never read my mother's books. I'm
>   told my father was really quite
>   remarkable during the last war. Best
>   parents I know.)

INT. STUDENT RESIDENCE. NIGHT

A six-bed sleeping quarters with the lights out. Zeffirelli and
Juliette sit cross-legged, naked, facing each other on the
sheets of a top bunk just below the ceiling. They talk rapidly
at a whisper, giggling, touching, sharing junk food and a Coke.
In the open bathroom door, a student in a dressing gown brushes
out her hair. Slowly: the interior background dissolves away
revealing stars, planets, the universe, infinity, etc. A tiny
comet inches across the sky-scape.

> ZEFFIRELLI (V.O.)
> The girls dormitory: first time I've come
> inside (except to vandalize it during
> demonstrations). I said, "Don't criticize
> my manifesto." She said, "Take off your
> clothes." I feel shy about my new
> muscles. Her large, stupid eyes watched
> me pee. A thousand kisses later: will she
> still remember the taste of my tool on
> the tip of her tongue? (Apologies, Mrs.
> Krementz: I know you despise crude
> language.)

INSERT:

Extreme close-up: the end of Zeffirelli's stray entry. Too
scribbly to read. Krementz's voice returns:

> KREMENTZ (V.O.)
> Additional sentence at bottom of page
> completely indecipherable due to poor
> penmanship.

INT. UNIVERSITY ROOFTOP. NIGHT

The tiny transmission booth next to the broadcasting tower above
the *quai*. Juliette, Vittel, Mitch-mitch, and the two other
headphoned student disc-jockeys sit clustered around Zeffirelli
(with an open, heavily-corrected-in-red-ink copy of the pink
pamphlet in his hands) at the microphone. The familiar French
pop song plays in the background as Zeffirelli announces to the
radio audience:

> ZEFFIRELLI
> "Revisions to a Manifesto." Page four,
> "Asterisk 1".

CUT TO:

An exterior view as Zeffirelli continues the broadcast
(inaudible through the sound-proof glass). Up above: an
electrical crackle and a bang/pop from the top of the broadcast
tower. A dust of falling sparks.

INSERT:

The "On Air" light flickers to "Off."

MONTAGE:

The listening audience at various radios: students at a
barricade, riot-police at an armored troop-transport, the
professor with his wife in curlers, Zeffirelli's sisters under a
sheet in their bedroom, Paul alone in his kitchen. They adjust
their dials, twist their antennae, poke, tap, shake, etc.

(Note: the audio track during the following sequence of shots
consists entirely of static interference, sizzling zaps,
oscillating warbles, and white noise. No live sound.)

CUT TO:

A high, direct-overhead, bird's-eye view of the transmission
booth. A hatch on the side cracks open, and Zeffirelli's head
pokes out and looks up at camera.

INSERT:

The top of the broadcasting tower. A science-project-type dry-
cell ignition battery (brand: *Éclair Blanche*) has been affixed
with duct tape and bailing wire to the side of the truss below a
whip antenna at the pinnacle of the structure. A pronged wire,
loosed from its terminal-post, dances, jolts, and flashes with
electrical arcs.

Zeffirelli reaches back inside and produces a pair of needle-
nose pliers. He says (silent):

                    ZEFFIRELLI
          Wait here.

Zeffirelli briskly, immediately, scales the tower, up out of
frame. Juliette, Mitch-mitch, and Vittel, alarmed, burst out of
the booth and shout urgently (silent) at Zeffirelli:

          VITTEL   MITCH-MITCH
Stop! What are you doing?   Are you crazy? Don't be
                                 stupid!

                    JULIETTE
          Come back down here right now,
          Zeffirelli!

Zeffirelli, cheerily ignoring his friends' warnings, reaches the
top of the flimsy broadcast tower. The structure bends and sways
slightly as he quickly pinches the prong of the live wire with
the pliers and re-inserts it into its terminal-post.

(Note: static ends, replaced by "Tip-top" with high-tenor vocals, expansive, orchestral backing, etc. Still no live sound.)

Juliette, Mitch-mitch, and Vittel stare up at Zeffirelli, tense with concern, involuntarily mouthing the words to the pop song. Zeffirelli waves down at them and gives a salute, reassuring, then looks out across the twinkling cityscape. He withdraws a fresh, skinny cigar from his breast pocket, holds it with the pliers, touches it to the gently sparking battery terminal, and puffs. He tucks the pliers under his belt. He smokes and smiles.

The battery explodes. A support cable snaps. Zeffirelli hangs on as the tower collapses.

INT. TAXI CAB. NIGHT

A Citroën sedan. Driver: woman, late middle-age, tired. The husband and wife (Zeffirelli's parents) sit together on one side of the back seat, arms intertwined, clasping hands, stone-faced. They wear pajamas/nightgown with belted overcoats. Krementz explains:

> KREMENTZ (V.O.)
> He is not an invincible comet speeding on
> its guided arc toward the outer reaches
> of the galaxy in cosmic space-time.
> Rather: he is a boy who will die young.
> He will drown on this planet, in the
> steady current of the deep, dirty,
> magnificent river that flows night and
> day through the veins and arteries of his
> own ancient city. His parents will
> receive a telephone call at midnight,
> dress briskly, mechanically, and hold
> hands in the silent taxi as they go to
> identify the body of their cold son.

The taxi stops. (A neon red cross glows outside the window.) The husband, startled, counts out coins from his pajama-top pocket. He and his wife exit. The *chauffeuse* drives on, passengerless.

> KREMENTZ (V.O.)
> His likeness (mass-produced and shrink-
> wrap packaged) will be sold like
> bubblegum to the hero-inspired -- who
> hope to see themselves like this:

MONTAGE:

A rapid-sequence of inserts. First: the original negative of a reportage photograph depicting Zeffirelli at chessboard, skinny cigar clenched in smiling teeth, dazzling/mischievious eyes flashing up to camera, caught mid-move as he slides his black

queen seven spaces, blurred by motion, to capture his rival's
white one. Filling the frame all around him: a platoon of armed
and armored standing riot-police. They react, gasping, groaning,
grimacing, wincing, etc.

Next: the same image (now a positive print) boxed in grease-
pencil on a contact sheet surrounded by the sequence of
exposures taken during the moments before/after.

Next: the front page of a newspaper with the same image (in
dotted halftone) and the caption below it: "Boy, skilled chess
player/activist in youth movement, dies."

Next: a snapshot of a gang of posing teenagers. One, front-and-
center, wears a T-shirt silk-screened with the same image.

Finally: a magazine advertisement using the same image
(airbrushed and colorized) to sell skinny cigars (branded:
"Toscano Zeffirelli").

EXT. RIVER EMBANKMENT. DAY

A crane on a barge alongside a footbridge clanks and ratchets as
it hoists the demolished broadcasting antenna out of the dark
water. An assembly of onlookers watches from the bank below a
street-sign: *Quai Blasé*.

INSERT:

A chessboard. It leans upright against the footbridge railing,
encircled with candles, flowers, paving-stones, scribbled
messages, a "Tip-top" record, and the above-mentioned clipping
(same image of Zeffirelli) held in place by a black queen as a
paperweight. Newsprint rustles slightly in the breeze.

                    KREMENTZ (V.O.)
        The touching narcissism of the young.

The camera dollies away from the impromptu shrine to reveal
Juliette (in Zeffirelli's transparent rain-slicker), Vittel (arm
in a sling), and Mitch-mitch (in National Duty-obligation
uniform, duffel over his shoulder) watching the river, backs to
camera, as the grey surface is peppered by a drizzling,
afternoon rain.

                    KREMENTZ (V.O.)
        March thirtieth.

INT. WALK-UP APARTMENT. DAY

Krementz's bedroom. On the television set: riot-police dismantle
abandoned barricades; firemen douse smoldering vehicles; a
milkman carries fresh bottles in two metal baskets. (A super-
title blinks: "Strikers Yield!")

                     KREMENTZ (V.O.)
              Across the street, a glaring metaphor:

Krementz (in her rose *peignoir*) sits up in bed, portable
typewriter on her knees, staring out the window. She wears the
gas-mask. Faint sound of shouting children in playground below.

                     KREMENTZ (V.O.)
              Bell rings; pupils scamper inside (back
              to their obedient classrooms); a creaky
              swing sways in the deserted schoolyard.

INT. WRITER'S OFFICE (KREMENTZ). DAY

Krementz sits alone at her desk eating burnt toast. A knock,
then the door creaks open, and Howitzer looks inside. Krementz
points at a manuscript on her desk. Howitzer enters and sits. He
reads, she eats.

Story #3
(pages 98 to 128)

INSERT:

The proof-print of a diner's chronicle in the Tastes and Smells
Section. A line-drawing depicts a dinner plate with a pen on one
side, a pencil and eraser on the other, and a ruled/margined
writing-paper placemat underneath.

TITLE:

>   Kitchen Accounts
>   "The Private Dining Room
>   of the Police Commissioner"
>   by Roebuck Wright

INT. TELEVISION STUDIO. DAY

The set of a talk show with three swivel-armchairs and an
ashtray on a pedestal. The host (white): forty, beige/check
three-piece, longish hair parted on the side. The guest (black):
fifty, open collar/silk scarf, burnt-orange safari suit. He is
Roebuck Wright. He speaks in the drawl (languid, literary) of
the Gothic American South. Both men smoke.

>   T.V. HOST
> Someone told me you have a photographic
> memory. Is that true?

>   ROEBUCK WRIGHT
> That is false. I have a typographic
> memory. I recollect the written word with
> considerable accuracy and detail -- but
> in other spheres my powers of retention
> are distinctly impressionistic. I am
> known to my intimates as a most forgetful
> man.

>   T.V. HOST
> Yet you remember every word you ever
> wrote: the novels, the essays, the poems,
> the plays --

>   ROEBUCK WRIGHT
>   (bittersweet)
> -- the unrequited valentines. Sadly, I
> do.

>   T.V. HOST
> May I test you?

>   ROEBUCK WRIGHT
>   (coy/demure)
> If you must.
>   (looking to audience)
> Unless we try the patience of your
>   (more)

                    ROEBUCK WRIGHT (cont'd)
          viewership --
                    (looking to wings)
          -- or the esteemed spokesmen of Gemini
          Toothpowder?

Off-stage: an actor stands at a sponsor display-table stacked
with tins of whitening dentifrice. He looks slightly startled,
then smiles awkwardly and nods. The host continues:

                    T.V. HOST
          My favorite piece is the one about the
          cook where the kidnappers get poisoned.

                    ROEBUCK WRIGHT
                    (immediately self-quoting)
          "Do students of the table dream in
          flavors?" This was the first of the
          questions a reporter for this magazine
          had diligently prepared in advance of his
          encounter with Lieutenant Nescaffier,
          ranking chef at District Headquarters on
          the narrow river-peninsula known as the
          Rognure d'Ongle. All such queries were to
          remain unanswered in the course of that
          eventful evening.
                    (brief pause)
          Shall I carry on?

                    T.V. HOST
                    (impressed)
          Please.

INT. GROUND-FLOOR HALLWAY. EVENING

A long, institutional-style corridor in a massive, seventeenth
century building. Dim overhead light. Worn, grey linoleum
floors. Dingy, chipped, cracked, yellowing, thick-gloss painted
walls. Camera leads Roebuck Wright (fifteen years younger,
dressed in a black suit and necktie) down the hall, shoes clip-
clopping, eyeballs searching left and right, lost.

                    ROEBUCK WRIGHT (V.O.)
          I had arrived insufficiently early.
          Though the suite of rooms on the
          penultimate floor of the grand edifice
          was hypothetically indicated on a
          floorplan provided on the back of the
          carte de dégustation --

INSERT:

Overhead angle: a slip of a paper pinched tightly in Roebuck
Wright's fingers. It is a menu for a nine course dinner with a
map (on the verso) of the labyrinthine compound.

CUT TO:

Roebuck Wright, same corridor. Camera now follows him.

>   ROEBUCK WRIGHT (V.O.)
>   -- it was nigh impossible to locate. At
>   least, for this reporter. (A weakness in
>   cartography: the curse of the
>   homosexual.)

Roebuck Wright makes a wrong turn, doubles-back, then U-turns,
repeatedly checking room numbers against his map.

>   ROEBUCK WRIGHT (V.O.)
>   M. Nescaffier made his name and
>   reputation (he is fanatically celebrated
>   among cooks, cops, and *capitains* -- not
>   to mention squealers, stoolies, and
>   snitches) as the great exemplar of the
>   mode of cuisine known as *Gastronomie*
>   *Gendarmique.*

MONTAGE:

Roebuck Wright pokes his head into the doorways of various
departmental offices. First: the crimes-in-progress dispatch
center (bank of phones, radio operator, wall map of the city
pocked with urgent alarms and alerts).

>   ROEBUCK WRIGHT (V.O.)
>   "Police cooking" began with the stake-out
>   picnic and paddy-wagon snack, but has
>   evolved and codified into something
>   refined, intensely nourishing, and, if
>   executed properly, marvelously flavorful.

Next: a training gymnasium with cadets in police-issue exercise
leotards performing fitness regimes (pugilist sparring, rope
climbing, medicine ball throwing).

>   ROEBUCK WRIGHT (V.O.)
>   Fundamentals: highly portable, rich in
>   protein, eaten with the non-dominant hand
>   only (the other being reserved for
>   firearms and paperwork).

Next: the target-end (bullets whizzing) of a marksmanship
practice range.

> ROEBUCK WRIGHT (V.O.)
> Most dishes are served pre-cut. Nothing
> crunchy. Quiet food.

Next: the disguises check-out dispensary (wigs, fake beards,
ecclesiastical vestments).

> ROEBUCK WRIGHT (V.O.)
> Sauces are dehydrated and ground to a
> powder to avoid spillage and the risk of
> the tainting of a crime scene.

Finally: an apparently unattended booking room. Roebuck Wright
pauses, momentarily mesmerized. He wanders slowly inside. He
stands at the door of a locked holding cell (hand-labeled
"Chicken Coop #1").

> ROEBUCK WRIGHT (V.O.)
> Diners are expected to provide their own
> *fourchettes de poche*, often engraved with
> the arcane mottoes and off-color sayings
> of their respective precincts.

A previously-unseen small, wiry, bespectacled number-cruncher
sleeping on a bunk inside the cell rustles slightly. Roebuck
Wright retreats a step, startled. The number-cruncher looks up
with frightened eyes. He says softly:

> NUMBER-CRUNCHER
> How are you planning to kill me?

> ROEBUCK WRIGHT
> (hesitates)
> I believe this to be a case of mistaken
> identity.

The number-cruncher looks skeptical. Roebuck Wright asks gently,
indicating the sign:

> ROEBUCK WRIGHT
> Have you been in the chicken coop for a
> very long while?

Off-screen: a theatrical cough/throat-clearing. Roebuck Wright
only now notices a previously-unseen platoon of guards (smoking,
snacking, reading, toothpicking, all armed with cylindrical-
magazine submachine guns) watching him evenly from around the
room. Roebuck Wright hesitates, apologetic.

> ROEBUCK WRIGHT
> I beg your pardon.

The number-cruncher watches, puzzled, as Roebuck Wright ducks
away. The camera booms down to the wooden baseboard below the
number-cruncher's bunk:

INSERT:

A spaghetti of carved graffiti. One message, only faintly
visible, seems to read: "Roebuck Wright was here."

CUT TO:

A narrow hallway on a high floor. A minuscule elevator on the
far end opens. Roebuck Wright emerges and approaches.

> ROEBUCK WRIGHT (V.O.)
> M. Nescaffier, even during his
> apprenticeship in a provincial fire
> department, aspired to a lofty perch, and
> there can be no higher position in the
> *métier* than that of *Chef Cuisinier* for
> the private dining room of the
> *Commissaire de la Police Municipale.*

The camera pans to a pair of double-doors discreetly labeled:
"Privé".

INT. DINING ROOM. NIGHT

The door creaks open and Roebuck Wright peers into:

A rustic, dark-wood chamber. Wide-plank floors. Low ceilings
supported by thick beams. Heavy, ornate, carved chairs and
sideboard. Lace curtains. Rugs in crimson. A carefully-set table
which seats: a sturdy but elegant eighty-year-old woman and two
fifty-five-year-old men. One is old for his age, bent, wrinkled,
ashen, and ghoulish. The other is young for his age, short
statured/broad shouldered, dressed in a well-tailored dark suit
with a shot of red thread sewn into the lapel. He is the
Commissaire. Across the room, next to a young policeman with an
apron over his uniform, a chef (French-Korean, tortoise-shell
spectacles, haircut with sharp bangs, fifty) stands lingering in
the kitchen doorway.

The entire group stares at camera/Roebuck Wright.

The *Commissaire* checks a clock on the mantelpiece (time: two
minutes after nine). He motions to a single, empty chair at the
table. Roebuck Wright, sheepish, approaches, sits, and says
gently:

> ROEBUCK WRIGHT
> Forgive my tardiness.

                         COMMISSAIRE
                       (suddenly warm)
          Not at all. Mr. Wright, may I present my
          mother, Louise de la Villatte. You can
          call her *Maman*. We all do.

Roebuck Wright bows to the old woman. Her smile exudes a
powerful maternal geniality. The *Commissaire* indicates the other
seated man:

                         COMMISSAIRE
          This is my oldest friend, *Chou-fleur*.
          When I met him, he was a girlish little
          schoolboy with ringlets and a full set of
          teeth. Now he looks like a corpse.

As the *Commissaire's* childhood friend chuckles to himself, his
dentures loudly click. Roebuck Wright bows again. The
Commissaire points across the room.

                         COMMISSAIRE
          In the corner, Patrolman Maupassant.
          He'll be serving.
                       (aside)
          Cocktails.

The patrolman/waiter briskly fetches up a tray of small aluminum
thermoses. He delivers them to the table just as a boy (French-
North African, age ten) in a blue lab coat enters through a side
door. He carries a carton filled with files and documents. He is
Gigi. A police academy cadet/nanny trails behind him. The
Commissaire, vaguely suspicious, explains as they pass:

                         COMMISSAIRE
          This is my son, Gigi, in the crime-lab
          smock. What are you stealing? From my
          personal records.

                         GIGI
          Unsolved cases.

                         COMMISSAIRE
          Say hello to Mr. Wright.

                         GIGI
          Hello, Mr. Wright.

                         ROEBUCK WRIGHT
          Hello, Gigi.

Gigi pauses to shake hands while balancing boxes. Roebuck Wright
explains in voiceover:

                    ROEBUCK WRIGHT (V.O.)
          Full name: Isadore Sharif de la Villatte.

FLASHBACK:

The *Commissaire* and a younger Gigi walk together down a dock
alongside the hull of an ocean liner. Stevedores hoist crates. A
mist drifts across the planks.

                    ROEBUCK WRIGHT (V.O.)
          The *Commissaire* and his only son,
          motherless and widowered, left the colony
          where the boy was born cemented together
          by their shared grief. Gigi was six.

The younger Gigi rides with his head sticking out the window of
a speeding police car. Sirens blast. The *Commissaire* is at the
wheel.

                    ROEBUCK WRIGHT (V.O.)
          His schoolrooms were the station house
          and the squad car.

The younger Gigi carefully presses the enormous, ink-coated
fingers of a hulking thug onto a blank arrest-form page. The
Commissaire (observing) looks pleased.

                    ROEBUCK WRIGHT (V.O.)
          He was educated by forensic tutors in the
          traditions of law enforcement.

A meek shopkeeper gives a description as the younger Gigi
finishes a sketch then flips it around to show: a wild-eyed,
crooked-toothed maniac. The shopkeeper nods. The *Commissaire*
(observing) looks pleased again.

                    ROEBUCK WRIGHT (V.O.)
          His first drawings were facial composites
          based on eyewitness testimony.

Split-screen: on the left, the younger Gigi taps a signal on a
telegraph machine; on the right, the *Commissaire* listens and
records.

                    ROEBUCK WRIGHT (V.O.)
          His first words were in Morse Code.

(Note: electronic beeps accompany a title sliding across the
bottom of the screen which reads: "*--* *- *--* *- P A P A".)

The younger Gigi and the *Commissaire* stand in front of the
crimes-in-progress wall map, studying alarms and alerts.

                    ROEBUCK WRIGHT (V.O.)
          It was, I suppose, wonderfully obvious.

Gigi and the *Commissaire* hold hands.

                    ROEBUCK WRIGHT (V.O.)
          He was brought up to succeed the
          Commissaire, himself.

CUT TO:

Gigi lingering next to Roebuck Wright. He says, pointed:

                    GIGI
          I've read you. In the magazine.

                    ROEBUCK WRIGHT
                    (hesitates)
          To your satisfaction?

                    GIGI
                    (broadly)
          Of course.

Gigi and his minder exit through a secret door into a cramped
spiral stairwell. The chef now stands at the elbow of the
Commissaire.

                    COMMISSAIRE
          I trust you're already familiar with this
          genius, at least by reputation:
                    (with pride, even vanity)
          Lieutenant Nescaffier.

                    ROEBUCK WRIGHT
                    (reverently)
          I surely am.

The party of four all look up to the chef. The chef salutes and
stands at ease, calm and confident. The *Commissaire* nods
"begin". The chef disappears. The diners unscrew their thermoses
and decant doses of a cloudy, lilac-colored liquid. They sip
their cocktails. Roebuck Wright, already enchanted, explains in
voiceover:

                    ROEBUCK WRIGHT (V.O.)
          The drink, a milky, purplish *aperitif*,
          ferociously fragrant, overtly medicinal,
          ever-so-faintly anesthetizing (and cooled
          to a glacial viscosity in a miniature
          version of the type of vacuum-flask
          normally associated with campsites and
          schoolrooms) cast a spell -- which,
          during the subsequent sixty second
                    (more)

                    ROEBUCK WRIGHT (V.O.) (cont'd)
          interval, was to be mortally broken. On
          three overlapping dramatic-timelines, the
          following events came to pass:

INSERT:

A black-gloved hand activates a stopwatch.

(Note: each segment of the following sequence portrays a
different scene occurring during the same approximately
simultaneous one-minute timespan, initiated by the same sound:
the stopwatch start. Loud ticking, amplified and reverberant,
continues throughout.)

MONTAGE:

1. In the kitchen: the chef blazes up an armory of cooktop-fires
and furnace-flames, then sets to work: chopping, stirring,
poaching, braising, flipping, folding, salting, spicing, etc.

                    ROEBUCK WRIGHT (V.O.)
          One. M. Nescaffier began his mysterious
          ritual. (I can neither comprehend nor
          describe what occurs behind a kitchen
          door. I have always been content to enjoy
          the issue of an artist's talent without
          unveiling the secrets of the chisel or
          the turpentine.)

2. In the nursery (a garret playroom decorated with books and
paints, trunks overflowing with costumes, a police rocking-
horse, etc.): Gigi and the cadet/nanny sit on tiny chairs at a
diminutive table as they examine the stacks of borrowed
paperwork.

                    ROEBUCK WRIGHT (V.O.)
          Two. The skylight window of the makeshift
          nursery which occupies the attic quarters
          jimmied ajar.

The camera tilts up to the vaulted glass ceiling. A pane inches
sideways in its frame with a nearly silent squeak. A black-
gloved hand gripping a medium-calibre automatic pistol (muzzle-
mounted with a silencer) cranes into the room. The extended
barrel slants toward the floor.

The camera tilts back down. The cadet/nanny stands up and exits
frame. He returns with an ashtray and lights a cigarette. He
puffs on it -- then, suddenly: he and Gigi both look to the
ceiling/skylight.

The camera tilts back up with a whip. The gun fires (a silencer
"thwoop"). Off-camera: a thump, a thud, and a thwack.

The camera tilts back down. The cadet/nanny is now dead in his tiny chair, shot through the top of the head, still bleeding liberally onto the strewn depositions etc. Gigi is gone.

A rope drops into frame from above. The chauffeur (a bent-nosed former heavyweight prize-fighter with a cauliflower ear and stitches on his forehead) who slides down and drops to the floor wears a grey cap; long, grey, double-breasted, black-belted coat; grey breeches; ballet slippers; and a white handkerchief tied over his face like a bandit. A coiled cord hangs over his shoulder. He darts/pads out of the shot. Off-camera: a scrambling hubbub.

The chauffeur re-enters carrying Gigi, trussed like a chicken, blindfolded, and gagged. He grips him at the waist. He takes a deep breath, bends his knees, then hurls the boy like a spinning circus tumbler straight up, through the ceiling skylight, out of the building. The chauffeur then takes the end of the rope and clips it to a metal ring strapped to his chest. He waits.

3. In the dining room: a small, red indicator-lightbulb mounted on the sideboard blinks on. The patrolman/waiter frowns slightly. He opens a cupboard door, withdraws a telephone, brings it to the dinner table, and plugs it into a socket flush-mounted on the burnished oak.

> ROEBUCK WRIGHT (V.O.)
> Three. Patrolman Maupassant, responding
> to an infrequently illuminated signal,
> delivered a telephone to his superior.

The *Commissaire* picks up the receiver and signals for his mother to pick up the extension.

> COMMISSAIRE
> Go ahead.

The *Commissaire* and his mother listen, stone-faced. She takes notes. Roebuck Wright exchanges an anxious look with *Chou-fleur*.

INSERT:

Maman's transcription (subtitled in English):

> As you know by now, we have kidnapped your son
> and absconded to a secure location which you
> will never discover. Release (or execute) the
> *Abacus*, and the little boy will be safely
> returned to your custody. Failure to do so by
> sun-up will result in your son's violent death.

The *Commissaire* hangs up, puzzled. He jolts to his feet and darts out of the room.

CUT TO:

A hand-drawn cel-animation shot vividly illustrating the rooftop of the *préfecture* headquarters in the bright moonlight. A stocky kidnapper is positioned next to the open skylight window. A thin kidnapper stands inside a large, black wicker basket.

>   ROEBUCK WRIGHT (V.O.)
>   The getaway (and eventual motor pursuit)
>   was rendered vividly (if, perhaps, a bit
>   fancifully) in a comic strip published
>   the following week.

The somersaulting boy (Gigi) flies up through the skylight. The stocky kidnapper catches him in his arms, quickly dumps him into the basket, and climbs in after. The thin kidnapper pulls a valve-chain, igniting a propane torch. The basket (now revealed in a slow zoom-out to be attached to a pitch black, stealth hot air balloon) rises -- carrying below it: the chauffeur, swaying gently as the balloon travels up and completely disappears into the night.

EXT. NARROW AVENUE. DAY

Early morning. A light snow falls on the doorstep of a low rent, residential hotel.

TITLE:

>   Three Days Earlier

The door opens, and the number-cruncher pokes out and looks up and down the sidewalk, nervous. He emerges in hat and overcoat carrying a yellow suitcase clutched to his chest. He walks briskly across the deserted street, through a narrow passageway, down an alley to: a parked, late forties (running boards, wire wheels) Citroën sedan. He gets in, tucks the suitcase beside him, and puts the key into the ignition. The motor whinnies, coughs, and sputters -- but fails to start. In the back seat, a policeman rises into view, pistol fixed on the back of the number-cruncher's head. The number-cruncher looks in the rearview mirror, then slowly raises his hands into the air. All around the vehicle: a dozen additional officers appear from behind and beneath various hiding places (trash can, window ledge, rain barrel, horse cart, coal chute). A paddy-wagon reverses into frame with a screech. The number-cruncher is whisked out of the Citroën, handcuffed, and swept up into the prisoner transport. A pair of iron doors slams shut.

                    ROEBUCK WRIGHT (V.O.)
     Though the infamous Ennui gang war
     "Winter Crimewave" had eradicated a
     healthy number of thugs and hooligans, it
     had also claimed the lives of a
     disgraceful proportion of innocent
     citizens. Due to the surprise capture of
     the racketeering accountant Albert the
     Abacus (in possession of a valise
     containing payroll stubs for all three of
     the city's major syndicates), the law-
     abiding community's hopes for an
     accelerated resolution to the crisis had
     been renewed. However: this turn of
     events had forcefully rattled the cages
     of the denizens of the criminal
     underworld.

Suddenly, a barrage of machine gun fire perforates the paddy-
wagon, the Citroën, the rain barrel, the horse cart, the coal
chute, most of the windows of the surrounding buildings, and the
bodies of a number of the assembled policemen. The surviving
officers return fire.

CUT TO:

The talk show. Roebuck Wright says, aside, to his host:

                    ROEBUCK WRIGHT
     For myself, I had failed to recognize the
     Abacus; but, as it happened: I knew the
     chicken coop. (This is not in the
     article, by the way.) If I refer to Mr.
     Howitzer, do you know who I mean?

                    T.V. HOST
     Of course.
          (to the audience)
     Arthur Howitzer, Jr. Founder and editor
     of "The French Dispatch".

                    ROEBUCK WRIGHT
     It was my first week in Ennui when I
     suffered the misfortune of being arrested
     in a drinking establishment on the
     fringes of the Flop Quarter (along with a
     number of newly-found companions).

                    T.V. HOST
     What was the charge?

                    ROEBUCK WRIGHT
          (simply)
     Love. You see, people may or may not be
               (more)

                    ROEBUCK WRIGHT (cont'd)
          mildly threatened by your anger, your
          hatred, your pride -- but love the wrong
          way: and you will find yourself in great
          jeopardy. In this case, a chicken coop
          jail cell for six days straight. I had no
          one who cared to rescue me, no one who
          cared to scold me, and the only local
          number committed to my typographic memory
          was:

INSERT:

A brief memo on "French Dispatch" letterhead. It reads (echoed
by Howitzer himself in voiceover):

          Dear Mr. Wright, While I regret we are unable to
          publish either of these specific pieces, I would
          be very pleased to consider other submissions in
          the future -- or, if you find yourself in Ennui:
          telephone me. You seem to know how to write.
          Signed, A.H. Jr.

Handwritten below the initials: the publisher's telephone
number.

                    ROEBUCK WRIGHT (V.O.)
          Printer's District 9-2211.

CUT TO:

The jail cell. Roebuck Wright (aged thirty) is now on the
inside: disheveled, unshaven, gaunt.

                    ROEBUCK WRIGHT (V.O.)
          I'd never met the man. I knew how to
          reach him only because I wanted a job.

A telephone slides through a meal-slot with a shlunk. Roebuck
Wright picks up the receiver and dials.

CUT TO:

A clock.

TITLE:

                    Thirty Minutes Later

The camera tilts down to reveal (on the other side of the iron
bars): Howitzer himself, seated on a folding chair, sipping a
cup of coffee. Roebuck Wright, inside his cell, fills out a
form, shakily, in pencil, on a clipboard. He finishes a last
sentence and slides the clipboard out the meal-slot. Howitzer
picks it up and studies the form.

> HOWITZER
> Let's see here.
> (muttering quickly)
> High school newspaper, poetry club, drama
> society...
> (clearly)
> Wrote the school song. Words and music.
> (muttering quickly)
> Junior researcher, cub reporter,
> assistant editor...
> (clearly)
> Fires and murders. That's how I started.
> My father owned the paper, of course.
> (muttering quickly)
> Bit of sports, bit of crime, bit of
> politics...
> (clearly)
> Shortlisted twice. For "Best Essays".
> (muttering)
> Deep South, Mid-west, East Coast...
> (clearly)
> Vast country. Haven't been there for
> twenty years.

A police guard appears with some paperwork to deliver to
Howitzer. He attempts to discreetly interrupt:

> POLICE GUARD
> Mr. Howitzer --

Howitzer responds sharply, holding up a finger:

> HOWITZER
> Not now. I'm conducting a job interview.

The guard freezes, then evaporates. Howitzer presses on,
shuffling pages:

> HOWITZER
> Your writing samples are good. I re-read
> them in the taxi. Ever done any book
> reviews?

> ROEBUCK WRIGHT
> (hesitates)
> Never.

> HOWITZER
> You're going to be here another few hours
> before they process you out. Read this --

Howitzer holds up a thin, hardback novel titled "Look Out
Below!". The dust-jacket illustration depicts a carbonated,
multicolored highball cocktail (bubbles, swizzle stick, lipstick

on the rim). A stamp on the cover reads: "Advance Copy".
Howitzer puts the book through the meal-slot.

> HOWITZER
> -- and give me 300 words. I'll pay you
> 500 francs, minus the 250 I advanced for
> your bail (but I'll re-advance half of
> that back to you for cost-of-living).
> Bring me a first draft tomorrow morning,
> and however you go about it, Mr. Wright:
> try to make it sound like you wrote it
> that way <u>on purpose</u>.

CUT TO:

Close-up, Roebuck Wright. There are tears in his eyes.

> ROEBUCK WRIGHT
> Thank you.

CUT TO:

Close-up, Howitzer. He says softly:

> HOWITZER
> No crying.

CUT TO:

The talk show. Roebuck Wright says, matter of fact:

> ROEBUCK WRIGHT
> He was to be my employer (and friend) for
> the next thirty years.
> (resumes self-quoting)
> It came to be known as the Night of a
> Thousand Slugs. (I'm reciting again.)

MONTAGE:

A succession of interrogations: a bare-knuckle beating in a
warehouse; a head plunged into a tub of ice; a face propelled
down the length of a bar, smashing through glasses, bottles, and
shakers; an upside-down thug swinging by his ankles from a meat
hook; a hulking goon with one eyelid swollen shut drowsily
watching a swinging pocket-watch; two policemen and a suspect
standing on a tarmac as an inert man is hurled from a low-flying
police airplane. The body bounces and tumbles to a bone-crunched
halt.

> ROEBUCK WRIGHT (V.O.)
> How the *Commissaire* and his elite team of
> experts and analysts succeeded so swiftly
> in determining the location of the
> (more)

                    ROEBUCK WRIGHT (V.O.) (cont'd)
              kidnappers' lair -- well, I just don't
              know. The tools of the trade, I suppose.

The suspect, in handcuffs, looks horrified. The two policemen
are stoic. One, notebook in hand, pencil poised, says:

                    POLICEMAN
              I'll repeat the question.

EXT. TENEMENT *HÔTEL*. NIGHT

A glowing window at the top-floor of a decrepit apartment
building.

                    ROEBUCK WRIGHT (V.O.)
              But succeed they did.

Six stories down the semi-crumbling facade, in the entry
passageway, a scrawny cat licks an empty saucer. The small,
cobblestone square in front, gas lamplit, is surrounded on all
sides by rickety buildings of cheap flats. Uneven, narrow, stone
staircases ascend from the street corners up to the higher,
encircling *rues* and *passages*. A footbridge edges one side of the
place, a train truss edges another. Cramped shops (closed) line
the sidewalks. Métro station: Hovel District.

Tucked and hidden around the corner: a dense cordon of officers,
squad cars, and paddy-wagons. A gathering crowd of locals (the
butcher, the fishmonger, the tobacconist, assorted neighborhood
characters) quietly nudge and jostle behind a police barrier.
Faintly heard, echoing across the *quartier*: a music hall.
Otherwise: silence.

A locksmith's shop serves as an improvised command center.
Ancient floor-plans and elevation-views, foxed and yellowed,
cover a long work-counter. A police-band radio hums and buzzes
while a voice broadcasts strategic instructions at a whisper.
The *Commissaire*, flanked by *Maman*, *Chou-fleur*, and Roebuck
Wright, peers out from the corner of a storefront window through
a pair of binoculars.

The camera pans/tilts up back to the glowing window at the top
of the decrepit building.

                    ROEBUCK WRIGHT (V.O.)
              Who were they? It was later revealed:

INT. TRIPLE APARTMENT. NIGHT

An expansive flat of small rooms, nooks/alcoves, and numerous
corridors which connect the top floors of various adjacent
buildings.

                    ROEBUCK WRIGHT (V.O.)
          A hired crew of bandits and gunmen
          imported by the ranking bosses of the
          Ennui rackets and their network of
          underworld middlemen.

In the sitting room: the chauffeur tunes and strums a guitar. In
the dining room: a stout man (cowboy hat, suit/necktie, dark
sunglasses) deals cards to a formidable, elderly woman. In the
kitchen: a scrawny thief tinkers with a dismantled radio. In the
corridor: a trio of hooligans of various dimensions stare into
space. In the bathroom: a quartet of showgirls bathe, paint
their toenails, and inject morphine. In front of a pad-locked
bedroom door: a pair of shoes (oxblood, lace up, the size of
Gigi's feet).

                    ROEBUCK WRIGHT (V.O.)
          Plus: one small, resourceful prisoner
          determined to free himself and reduce
          taxpayer expense.

INSERT:

Gigi's bound hands in dim near-blackness. His fingers clink a
beat on a tarnished conduit with a half-*centime* coin.

INT/EXT. LAUNDRY CLOSET. NIGHT

Split-screen. On the right, Gigi in a chair, tied up in a dark
cupboard. On the left, one of the junkie showgirls, wrapped in a
towel, frowning and listening, as she inclines toward the
padlocked door. She chews gum.

                    SHOWGIRL
          What's that noise?

Gigi stops clinking. A beat.

                    GIGI
          Air bubbles in the radiator pipes. It's
          pressurized.

                    SHOWGIRL
          Sounds like Morse Code.

                    GIGI
                (vaguely)
          Vaguely. I'm Gigi, by the way. What's
          your name?

                    SHOWGIRL
          I'm not going to tell you that. This is a
          felony.

                         GIGI
                      (defiant)
             You're not a criminal. You're just a
             mixed-up showgirl.

                       SHOWGIRL
             Ha.

                         GIGI
             Ha, yourself.

Pause. Gigi switches gears:

                         GIGI
             Are you hungry? I can hear your stomach
             growling.

Pause. Gigi tries once more:

                         GIGI
             Sing me a lullaby. I'm scared.

                       SHOWGIRL
             No.

Another pause. The showgirl sings a lullaby. She sighs.

                       SHOWGIRL
             Are you asleep?

                         GIGI
                      (quietly)
             Yes.

INSERT:

The *Commissaire's* hand. He fingers a miniature cameo locket
which displays a photograph of the younger Gigi.

                   ROEBUCK WRIGHT (V.O.)
             The *Commissaire* adored Gigi with all his
             voluminous heart.

The *Commissaire* paces up and down the room, fretting and
contemplating.

                   ROEBUCK WRIGHT (V.O.)
             However: his <u>mind</u> (that exceptional
             machine for the detection and
             investigation of criminal activity) had
             been whirring since dinnertime, and he
             was in a condition of dire calorific
             depletion.

The *Commissaire* stops and murmurs, finally giving in:

> COMMISSAIRE
> *Maman*? I'm hungry.

Maman (who has clearly been waiting for this moment) immediately signals to an off-screen attendant and produces a collapsible pocket-fork, which she unfolds. The *Commissaire* and *Chou-fleur* follow suit. The patrolman/waiter swiftly covers a workbench below the front window end-to-end with a checkered tablecloth.

The camera dollies away, into the back room (normally a die-casting and lathing workshop), which has been converted into a temporary kitchen. A sheet of pastries warms over a bank of emergency candles. A tray of shucked oysters cools over a bed of dry ice. Small pots boil along radiator pipes. Meat and fowl in states of mid-preparation hang from the ceiling in nets and baskets. Portable ovens and bunsen burners glow and flicker at lowest flame. Nescaffier whisks a froth in a bowl at a perfectly continuous, robotic rate.

> ROEBUCK WRIGHT (V.O.)
> Nescaffier, back in the field for the
> first time in six years, came prepared to
> dazzle.

The patrolman/waiter pokes his head into the room and nods.

> ROEBUCK WRIGHT (V.O.)
> The change was instantaneous.

EXT. LOCKSMITH SHOP. NIGHT

The congregation of police and bystanders outside wait in respectful silence while, seated in the window, behind a pulled blind, in silhouette: the *Commissaire, Maman, Chou-fleur*, and Roebuck Wright all watch Nescaffier's shadow enter carrying a serving tray. The *Commissaire* rises to his feet and wafts the scent into his nose.

> ROEBUCK WRIGHT (V.O.)
> Even as the faintest hints of the aromas
> of the great chef's kitchen ribboned into
> the *Commissaire's* nostrils, he began to
> envision and formulate a multi-pronged
> battle-plan.

MONTAGE:

Split-screen: on the right, the *Commissaire,* seated at the workbench table in the locksmith shop, speaks excitedly to *Chou-fleur* while eating continuously with his left hand only; on the left, a small, speckled, boiled egg split open to reveal layers of whipped yolk *mousse.*

ROEBUCK WRIGHT (V.O.)
To start: deviled eggs of the precinct canary served in shells of its own meringue.

COMMISSAIRE
Send a commando unit to secure all access points to the south and west.

On the right, the *Commissaire,* seated at the workbench table in the locksmith shop, speaks excitedly to *Maman* while eating continuously with his left hand only; on the left: a saucer of *gibiers* and *fruits des bois.*

ROEBUCK WRIGHT (V.O.)
Next: kidneys poached with plums from the mayor's rooftop arbor.

COMMISSAIRE
Send a guerrilla detachment to block all egress routes to the east and north.

On the right, the *Commissaire* illustrates (using arrows and X's) his scheme/strategy on one of the building floor plan maps; on the left, small *boulettes* shaped and packaged like a bowl of candies.

ROEBUCK WRIGHT (V.O.)
Then: minced lamb *bon-bons* in pastry wrappers.

COMMISSAIRE (V.O.)
Drill tunnels (circumference: 75mm) through the partition walls of all three adjacent buildings.

On the right, teenage boys and girls in shooting costumes perch among high chimney tops; on the left, another thermos.

ROEBUCK WRIGHT (V.O.)
Blasé oyster soup.

COMMISSAIRE (V.O.)
On the rooftops: amateur snipers from the local hunting club.

On the right, a quartet of gear-laden climbers in lederhosen scramble in formation up a dark alley; on the left: a roasted bird, boneless, bloody, chopped with potatoes, and served in a paper cup.

ROEBUCK WRIGHT (V.O.)
A magnificent city-park pigeon hash.

COMMISSAIRE (V.O.)
Down the elevator shaft: amateur climbers from the district Alpinist society.

On the right, a light clicks on as an enormous wrestler (in a striped singlet) is awakened from slumber by a ringing telephone; on the left, a nicotine *pot de crème* with a white blob on top.

ROEBUCK WRIGHT (V.O.)
Finally: *tabac* pudding with quadruple cream.

COMMISSAIRE (V.O.)
Wake up the *Jeroboam,* too. I want him limber, just in case.

CUT TO:

The talk show (once again). The host gently cuts in:

                    T.V. HOST
          May I interrupt? With a question.

                    ROEBUCK WRIGHT
          Please. Just permit me to dog-ear the
          page. Mentally.

          T.V. HOST   ROEBUCK WRIGHT
Forgive me. I beg your pardon.   Heavens, no. Whatever for?

                    ROEBUCK WRIGHT
          Ready.

                    T.V. HOST
          You've written about the American negro,
          the French intellectual, the Southern
          romantic; scripture, mythology, folklore;
          true crime, false crime; the ghost story,
          the picaresque, the *bildungsroman* -- but,
          more than anything, over all these years:
          you've written about food. Why?

Roebuck Wright stiffens and crosses his arms snugly across his
chest. Pause. He counts with five fingers:

                    ROEBUCK WRIGHT
          Who? What? Where? When? How. Valid
          questions -- but I learned as a cub
          stringer: never, under any circumstance,
          if it is remotely within your power to
          resist the impulse, never ask a man <u>why</u>.
          It tightens the fellow up.
                    (referring to his own posture)
          Look at me.

                    T.V. HOST
                    (hesitates)
          I apologize: but I'm going to hold you to
          it --

                    ROEBUCK WRIGHT
          Torture.

          T.V. HOST   ROEBUCK WRIGHT
-- if you'll allow me.   (Self-reflection is a vice
                                best conducted in private or
                                not at all.)

                    ROEBUCK WRIGHT
          Well, I'll answer the question, out of
          sheer weariness, but I truly don't know
          what I'm about to say.

Silence. Roebuck Wright's arms drop. He sighs deeply and speaks from some new chamber of his mind/heart:

> ROEBUCK WRIGHT
> There is a particular, sad beauty well-known to the companionless foreigner as he walks the streets of his adopted (preferably, moonlit) city. (In my case, Ennui, France.) I have so often shared the day's glittering discoveries with: no one at all. But always, somewhere along the avenue or the boulevard: there was a table. Set for me. A cook, a waiter, a bottle, a glass, a fire. I chose this life. It is the solitary feast that has been (very much like a comrade) my great comfort and fortification.

A tear (perhaps) rolls down Roebuck Wright's cheek. The T.V. host produces a clean handkerchief and offers it. Roebuck Wright laughs (almost silently) and rolls his eyes as he takes it.

> T.V. HOST
> Do you remember where you placed the bookmark?

> ROEBUCK WRIGHT
> Of course. "Meanwhile."
> (back to the story)
> Meanwhile, across the street:

CUT TO:

The radio, partially reassembled. It crackles to life. A broadcast voice whispers:

> POLICE BANDWIDTH
> *Be informed: suspects' lair is top floor, lower edge of square; officers are already in place around perimeter and surrounding rooftops; maintain extreme discretion and caution approaching location. Repeat...*

The scrawny thief scrambles out of the kitchen, jolts into the front window, and pulls the curtains slightly ajar. The other members of the gang instinctively flock around him to look out, as well.

CUT TO:

The gang's point-of-view of the square below: empty. Silence. A single cigarette flicks through the air from behind a corner and sparks onto the cobblestones.

The chauffeur squints.

CUT TO:

The *Commissaire* monitoring the radio. He has a sudden intuition. He peers under the locksmith's blinds. From the top floor flat: one first bang, then a storm of gunfire.

CUT TO:

Inside the lair. The apartment has been flash-converted into a fortress/armory. Pistols, rifles, a machine gun on a tripod, plus a military ordnance grenade launcher. Everyone (chauffeur, Stetson, spinster, showgirls, thugs, thief) blasts away at the square below.

Every window shatters. Bricks and mortar explode. Vehicles are blown to smithereens. The teenage snipers shoot back from the rooftops. Police duck for cover. Blood, smoke, falling bodies, screaming, etc.

The *Commissaire*, on the floor of the locksmith shop, showered in shards and splinters (with his mother, his best friend, and our reporter) repeats over and over into the radio microphone:

> COMMISSAIRE
> Hold your fire! Hold your fire! Hold your
> fire!

CUT TO:

A tiny, old man in a mezzanine listening keenly at a radiator down-pipe while the bullets bang and ricochet outside. He puts on a stethoscope, holds it against the tarnished brass, and begins to take notes.

> ROEBUCK WRIGHT (V.O.)
> During a lull in the skirmish, an ancient
> concierge, veteran of two wars, limped
> across the street to deliver an enigmatic
> message.

INSERT:

A scrap of graph paper studded with dots and dashes and a translation below: "S E N D   T H E   C O O K".

INT. LOCKSMITH SHOP. NIGHT

Above the counter: a final lightbulb pops (gunshot). Silence.

TITLE:

One Hour Later

CUT TO:

The scarred and battered square. The *Commissaire,* hands in the air, steps carefully into view. He carries a loudspeaker. His voice reverberates across the square:

> COMMISSAIRE
> I'm speaking to the leader of the gang of kidnappers on the top floor.

No response. The *Commissaire* continues:

> COMMISSAIRE
> Do you have a working kitchen in your lair?

No response. The *Commissaire* continues:

> COMMISSAIRE
> My son needs a snack. Allow us to send in our precinct cook along with some supplies and provisions. He will prepare a supper of sufficient proportions to feed you and all your accomplices. (We already ate.)

CUT TO:

The gang conferring all at once at a murmur ("Of course not!" "Are they kidding?" "They think we're stupid." etc.) until the chauffeur has a realization. He leans slightly in front of the window and shouts:

> CHAUFFEUR
> Is it an underling -- or Nescaffier himself?

The *Commissaire* gives a signal. Nescaffier appears. He salutes up to the unseen kidnappers. Aside: he and the *Commissaire* exchange a look of grim defiance (and fear).

INT. SERVICE STAIRS. NIGHT

Nescaffier, cast in dark shadow, carries a short tower of boxes and cartons (meat, produce, bread, butter, etc.) as he calmly ascends the winding steps. On top of the stack: a bowl of radishes -- which appear to glow in the darkness.

INT. KITCHEN. NIGHT

The gang sits on chairs and stools crowded around a breakfast table set with nine identical dinners on segmented, prison-style

plates: a savory winter tart, *purée*, vivid greens, radishes. Two
more plates rest on the sideboard. Nescaffier stands apart,
hands folded, apron splattered. In the background: the stove,
oven, and sink are a battleground strewn with pots, pans,
knives, spoons, etc. In the next room: the thief watches the
street from the machine gun's telescopic sight.

Nescaffier explains humbly:

> NESCAFFIER
> Blackbird pie.

Nescaffier backs away slightly.

The chauffeur holds up his finger: wait. He quickly prepares a
small side-dish with a taste of each item from his own plate and
those of the thug and spinster on either side of him. He hands
the dish to Nescaffier.

The gang watches as Nescaffier, without hesitation, takes out
his own *fourchette de poche* and eats everything -- including,
finally, a single radish.

> ROEBUCK WRIGHT (V.O.)
> Required, of course, to sample each item,
> the chef ate the deathly poison --

The thief appears in the doorway to collect his plate, one of
the showgirls (murmuring: "for the little boy") carries another
plate down the corridor, and the rest of the gang attacks their
dinners.

The chauffeur pauses suddenly. The others hesitate, watching.
The chauffeur says crisply to Nescaffier:

> CHAUFFEUR
> Write down the recipe.

Nescaffier nods, and they all continue their voracious grazing.

CUT TO:

The lair as it is breached all at once from three directions: a
large hole blasts through one wall, a large drill ruptures
through another, the Alpinists drop from a trap door in the
ceiling. The apartment fills with climbers and commandos. They
all freeze.

> ROEBUCK WRIGHT (V.O.)
> -- but Nescaffier survived: thanks to the
> extreme fortitude (bolstered and braced,
> season upon season, by the richest, most
> potent plates, pans, and sauce pots) of
> his almost superhuman stomach.

Strewn across the floor: dead kidnappers and empty plates.
Nescaffier lies -- half-unconscious, shivering, but alive --
among them. The commandos immediately jump to his aid, injecting
him with three pre-loaded syringes of brightly colored medicine,
slipping a tube down his throat, pipetting droplets into his
eyes, massaging arms, legs, heart. As they continue these
ministrations, the camera moves out of the room, down the
corridor, to the open closet door. On the floor: another plate,
not quite empty. A trio of radishes remains.

>   ROEBUCK WRIGHT (V.O.)
>   He knew well, of course: Gigi loathed and
>   despised the radish in all its forms with
>   a deep, unbridled passion, and had never
>   so much as touched one (or even spoken
>   the word) during his entire young
>   lifetime.

Across the room: one more plate, also with a handful of leftover
radishes on it.

>   ROEBUCK WRIGHT (V.O.)
>   However, as it happened, the chauffeur
>   hated radishes, too.

Outside: an alarm bell rings. The commandos run to the window
and look down into the square.

(Note: the following sequence is rendered entirely in the same
hand-drawn cel-animation method and style previously established
for the hot air balloon getaway.)

CUT TO:

The commandos' P.O.V: straight down from the window looking at
the square. The courtyard gate bursts open, and a two-door
Citroën sedan (chauffeur at wheel, Gigi beside him) roars out
into the square, smashing through barricades and scattering the
crowd of officers and onlookers before rumbling away up a blind
impasse under the street-sign: "Pick-pocket Cul-de-Sac.

The *Commissaire, Maman, Chou-fleur*, and Roebuck Wright scramble
out of the locksmith shop and leap into their own Citroën. The
Commissaire cranks the motor. It stutters.

After a double-circling U-turn: the chauffeur and Gigi's Citroën
comes squealing and careening from the cul-de-sac back into the
square. The wrestler springs out of a paddy-wagon, side-steps in
front of the weaving vehicle, and hurtles himself onto the hood
with a whang. The chauffeur looks shocked. Gigi looks ecstatic.
The wrestler rips off the windshield wipers and attempts to pull
the car apart while also struggling desperately not to fall off.
The chauffeur accelerates through a corner and up a different
road.

The *Commissaire* gets the engine going and slams his foot down on the gas pedal, revving up in pursuit of the other vehicle.

Narrow streets. Twisty corners. A tunnel and a bridge. The two cars scream through the sleeping city. At the top of a hill: the chauffeur skids to a stop and jumps out (with the bound Gigi tucked under his arm). He sprints away down a staircase. The wrestler runs after him.

The *Commissaire* jolts to a stop behind the other car. He and Roebuck Wright bounce out and run after the others (*Maman* and *Chou-fleur* stay behind).

A high-speed foot chase takes them down a drainpipe, across a catwalk, under a scaffolding, over a stone wall -- then back up to the parked cars. The chauffeur shoots back into the driver's seat and guns the engine. Just as he tears away, the wrestler manages to jump back onto the hood, furious. The *Commissaire* and Roebuck Wright rejoin *Maman* and *Chou-fleur*, and the car chase resumes.

On a long straightaway: Gigi suddenly pokes up his head from his car's canvas sunroof. He finishes unscrambling the bindings around his arms, and his hands are free. The chauffeur attempts to grab at Gigi while still piloting the Citroën. The *Commissaire* shouts to Roebuck Wright:

> COMMISSAIRE
> Take the wheel!

The *Commissaire* climbs out the window of the racing vehicle and crawls onto the hood. Roebuck Wright, horrified, lunges into the driver's seat. Gigi pops out fully onto the roof of the other car, then leaps from one moving vehicle back toward the other, sailing through the air, arms and legs splayed -- into his father's arms. They are both knocked back smashing into the windshield (which cracks), then tumble up onto the rooftop and slash down through their own ripping canvas sunroof into the laps of *Maman* and *Chou-fleur*.

The chauffeur misjudges the next turn, slides off the street, cracks through a guardrail, flies bashing into a dry riverbed, and explodes into a spectacular fireball. The wrestler tumbles to safety and lands in "neutral position".

> ROEBUCK WRIGHT (V.O.)
> Perhaps the most stirring (and startling)
> phenomenon witnessed over the trajectory
> of that protracted dinner date was this:

In the back seat: Gigi slaps his father hard across the face. The *Commissaire's* hat, glasses, cigarette, hairpiece, and eyebrows all fly off his head in different directions. The *Commissaire* looks astonished, Gigi looks shocked. The

Commissaire quickly re-attaches his false eyebrows -- then both begin to simultaneously laugh and cry. They kiss and embrace.

(Note: resume live-action.)

EXT. POLICE HEADQUARTERS. DAY

A troop of armed police escort a plainclothesman -- carrying the number-cruncher's yellow suitcase handcuffed to his wrist -- across a street to an armored transport. The plainclothesman trips on the curb, the suitcase snaps open, and the air instantly fills with fluttering documents which confetti into an expanding cloud out over the banks of the river.

> ROEBUCK WRIGHT (V.O.)
> Often, in fiction, the illicit treasure
> which has cost and destroyed so many
> lives is finally plucked away by the hand
> of destiny, vaporized into smoke,
> dispersed to the winds, etc. This did not
> occur.

The camera booms down below the sidewalk to glimpse an endless underground cache of anonymous file cabinets and forgotten storage boxes. The briefest pause, then the camera booms back up to the cloud of papers.

> ROEBUCK WRIGHT (V.O.)
> The pay stubs remain sealed in a humidity-
> controlled, underground evidence vault;
> but: in light of the judicial ruling (due
> to bribery) which declared the entire
> trove legally inadmissible --

The camera booms back up to the cloud of papers.

> ROEBUCK WRIGHT (V.O.)
> -- this staged imagining does seem
> appropriate in its depiction of a grand,
> thematic pointlessness.

INT. JAIL CELL. DAY

The number-cruncher, still behind bars, eats his breakfast. He looks happy. Seated outside the cell, still connected to a rolling I.V. drip but only slightly the worse for wear, Nescaffier watches and pours himself a glass of the lilac-colored *aperitif* (from a thermos, of course).

> ROEBUCK WRIGHT
> A delicious irony: M. Albert, accountant
> to the *demi-monde* and remote cause of the
> entire spectacular contretemps, had been
> entirely forgotten in the chicken coop
> (more)

             ROEBUCK WRIGHT (cont'd)
from Thursday dinner to Monday breakfast
and had very nearly starved in his cell.
It was only the convalescent M.
Nescaffier himself who retained the
presence of mind to prepare the prisoner
an *omelette à la policier* which he
delivered warm, wrapped in a day-old
search warrant.

INT. TELEVISION STUDIO. DAY

Back on the talk show, Roebuck Wright concludes:

             ROEBUCK WRIGHT
The *Abacus* ate well that morning.

Silence. The host, respectful, turns to camera.

             T.V. HOST
A word from Gemini Toothpowder.

INT. WRITER'S OFFICE (ROEBUCK WRIGHT). DAY

On the daybed: Roebuck Wright reposes, smoking, hands folded
across his lap. In the corner: the cheery writer reads a pocket
atlas and eats breadsticks. At the desk: Howitzer, feet on the
table, flips through out-of-order pages. He grumbles:

             HOWITZER
It was supposed to be an article about a
great chef.

             ROEBUCK WRIGHT
          (untroubled)
It is. In part.

             HOWITZER
For the Tastes and Smells section.

             ROEBUCK WRIGHT
I understand. The assignment was
perfectly clear. Perhaps you fail to
grasp: I was shot at and hand grenaded
<u>against</u> my will. I only asked to be <u>fed</u>
(and <u>was</u>, marvelously, as I describe in
some detail).

             HOWITZER
          (doubtful)
Nescaffier only gets one line of
dialogue.

                    ROEBUCK WRIGHT
                  (long pause)
          Well, I did <u>cut</u> something he told me. It
          made me too sad. I could stick it back
          in, if you like.

                    HOWITZER
                  (guardedly optimistic)
          What'd he say?

Roebuck Wright floats to the wastebasket, digs briefly, and
withdraws a single, crumpled page. He tosses it, underhand, to
Howitzer, who snatches it out of the air and snaps it open in
one motion.

EXT. LOCKSMITH SHOP. NIGHT

Over the street gutter: the shrouded bodies of the dead
kidnappers rest in a neat row along the cobblestones. Below a
streetlamp: the *Commissaire* clutches Gigi at his side as he
addresses members of the press. Under a white tent: Nescaffier,
on a gurney, eyes closed, continues to receive intravenous
medication. Roebuck Wright sits next to him on a stool.

Suddenly: Nescaffier speaks:

                    NESCAFFIER
          They had a flavor.

                    ROEBUCK WRIGHT
                  (hesitates)
          I beg your pardon?

                    NESCAFFIER
          The toxic salts. In the radishes. They
          had a flavor. Totally unfamiliar to me.
          Like a bitter, moldy, peppery, spicy,
          oily kind of -- earth. I never tasted
          that taste in my life. Not very pleasant,
          extremely poisonous, but still: a new
          flavor. That's a rare thing, at my age.

                    ROEBUCK WRIGHT
                  (pause)
          I admire your bravery, Lieutenant.

                    NESCAFFIER
                  (genuinely)
          I'm not brave. I just wasn't in the mood
          to be a disappointment to everybody.
                  (in explanation)
          I'm a foreigner, you know.

                    ROEBUCK WRIGHT
                  (long pause)
       This city is full of us, isn't it? I'm
       one, myself.

Nescaffier is aware of this. He says, slightly delirious:

                    NESCAFFIER
       Seeking something missing. Missing
       something left behind.

Roebuck Wright nods in appreciation. He says quietly:

                    ROEBUCK WRIGHT
       Maybe, with good luck, we'll find what
       eluded us in the places we once called
       home.

Nescaffier smiles sadly and shakes his head: no.

CUT TO:

Howitzer and Roebuck Wright. Howitzer says, pleased/annoyed:

                    HOWITZER
       That's the best part of the whole thing.
       That's the <u>reason</u> for it to be written.

                    ROEBUCK WRIGHT
              (flattered/irritated)
       I couldn't agree less.

                    HOWITZER
              (hesitates)
       Well, anyway, don't cut it.

Postscript
(pages 130 to 132)

INT. EDITORIAL OFFICE. EVENING

On a table: the proofreader. On the couch: the story editor and
legal advisor. In the corner: the cheery writer. Also: Berensen,
Sazerac, Krementz. The copy boy (lingering near the door,
apparently still employed at the magazine) has tears on his face
again -- but, it appears: so does everyone else.

The door opens, and Roebuck Wright enters. He stands, frozen,
staring across the room. The alumna looks up from her spiral
bound notebook.

                    ALUMNA
          Are we all here? I guess you know. It was
          a heart attack. He's dead.

On the desk: Howitzer's body, under a tablecloth, surrounded by
a multitude of strewn telegrams. A bearded doctor takes off his
stethoscope and tucks it into a bag resting on the chest of the
corpse.

                    DOCTOR
          Excuse me.

The doctor takes the bag and exits. The alumna grits her teeth,
fighting herself -- then, suddenly: she is sobbing. Berensen
grips her arm to comfort her (a bit stern). Krementz points
above the door and says simply:

                    KREMENTZ
          No crying.

The alumna immediately stops crying. She takes a deep breath.
Roebuck Wright folds back the upper edge of the tablecloth,
looks down at Howitzer's face (peaceful) for a moment, then
covers him up again. The cheery writer asks grimly:

                    CHEERY WRITER
          Is somebody coming to take him away?

The legal advisor checks his watch. He explains:

                    LEGAL ADVISOR
          There's a strike at the morgue.

In the next room (seen through a glass partition): the doctor
makes arrangements on the telephone. The usual waiter enters
carrying an American-style birthday cake. He hesitates. Roebuck
Wright asks, hands on Howitzer's shoulders:

                    ROEBUCK WRIGHT
          Who was with him?

STORY EDITOR
He was alone. Reading birthday telegrams.

The waiter places the cake onto the table and lights a match.
Krementz interrupts with a blunt:

KREMENTZ
Don't light the candles. He's dead.

Pause. The waiter blows out the match. Sazerac murmurs sadly:

SAZERAC
I'll have a slice.

The waiter prepares cake for Sazerac. Roebuck Wright gestures:
just a sliver for me. The alumna pulls herself together.

ALUMNA
We need to draft something. Who wants it?

The proofreader scribbles on a chit, snaps her fingers, and
passes the chit to the copy boy as she explains:

PROOFREADER
We've got a file.

The copy boy dashes out the door. Hermès Jones, doodling on a
paper napkin, announces:

HERMÈS JONES
I'm working on the art.

INSERT:

The coffee-stain and *confiture* caricature of Howitzer seen at
the start of the film, two-thirds finished.

Sazerac studies the picture. He smiles.

SAZERAC
That's him.

Roebuck Wright turns on an electric typewriter (next to the
deceased) as he says, including all the assembled reporters:

ROEBUCK WRIGHT
Let's write it together.

The writers variously: push back from their tables, fold their
hands in their laps, look up toward the ceiling, look off into
space, etc. as they begin to mentally outline the story. The
waiter asks, puzzled:

                    WAITER
          Write what?

                    ALUMNA
          The obituary.

The waiter nods, finally understanding. The copy boy returns
with a folder which he unfolds on the desk. Roebuck Wright types
as he dictates:

                    ROEBUCK WRIGHT
          Arthur Howitzer, Jr. Born in North
          Kansas, ten miles from the geographical
          center of the United States.

                    ALUMNA
          Mother died when he was five.

                    STORY EDITOR
          Son of a newspaper publisher, founder of
          this magazine.

                    BERENSEN
          "The French Dispatch". Previously known
          as "Picnic".

                    KREMENTZ
          A largely unread Sunday supplement to the
          Liberty, Kansas Evening Sun.

                    SAZERAC
          It began as a holiday.

                    HERMÈS JONES
          Is that true?

                    SAZERAC
          Sort of.

Mumbling and sad laughter. Roebuck Wright says finally:

                    ROEBUCK WRIGHT
          What happens next?

CUT TO:

The office from the next room (seen through the glass
partition). Roebuck Wright resumes typing, and the writers and
staff, gathering closer around him, continue to remember and
recount.

THE FRENCH DISPATCH

Gallery of images